BREACH OF PROMISE TO MARRY

A HISTORY OF HOW JILTED BRIDES SETTLED SCORES

PEN & SWORD HISTORY

First published in 2014 by

an imprint of
Pen & Sword Books Ltd
47 Church Street
Barnsley
South Yorkshire
S70 2AS

ISBN:- 9781783030361

Printed and bound in the UK by CPI Group (UK) Ltd,
Croydon, CRO 4YY

Pen & Sword Books Ltd incorporates the imprints of Pen &
Sword Archaeology, Atlas, Aviation, Battleground, Discovery,
Family History, History, Maritime, Military, Naval, Politics,
Railways, Select, Social History, Transport, True Crime, and
Claymore Press, Frontline Books, Leo Cooper, Praetorian Press,
Remember When, Seaforth Publishing and Wharncliffe.

For a complete list of Pen & Sword titles please contact

PEN & SWORD BOOKS LIMITED

47 Church Street, Barnsley, South Yorkshire, S70 2AS, England
E-mail: enquiries@pen-and-sword.co.uk
Website: www.pen-and-sword.co.uk

BREACH OF PROMISE TO MARRY

A HISTORY OF HOW JILTED BRIDES SETTLED SCORES

Denise Bates

Remembering
Colin Marshall, Kathleen Wordsworth (née Marshall)
and Frank Wordsworth,
my lovely aunty and two wonderful uncles

Contents

Introduction

Breach of promise of marriage was an unusual law allowing a jilted person to obtain damages from an intended husband or wife who had then refused to marry them. It developed in the last decades of the eighteenth century, enjoyed its heyday during Queen Victoria's reign, and gradually became an anachronism in the twentieth century as the social assumptions upon which it was based changed for ever. Few tears were shed when the claim was finally abolished in 1970.

Less than 50 years later, the social and cultural phenomenon that was breach of promise has almost disappeared from view, intruding only occasionally in a handful of nineteenth century novels and theatrical works which have stood the test of time. Yet Dickens's tragic, melodramatic Miss Havisham, his comical, naïve Mr Pickwick, the grasping, amoral Angelina in Gilbert and Sullivan's *Trial by Jury* and Vesta Victoria's music-hall song about a jilted woman left *'waiting at the church'* are unrepresentative portraits of the social influence of breach of promise.

As I began to look at the real plaintiffs and defendants in breach of promise cases, how a claim could change lives for better or worse and why cross-class romances were frowned on in Victorian society, I stumbled upon a claim which reveals timeless aspects of human nature, such as greed, selfishness, revenge and immaturity. Virtuous maidens, unmarried mothers, embittered spinsters and career fraudsters jostle alongside no-win-no-fee lawyers, love-'em-and-leave-'em seducers, naïve young men and ageing Lotharios in a canvas that seems more like a Hogarth caricature sprung to life than a lovelorn lady nursing a broken heart.

Breach of promise was predominantly a woman's action. Men were entitled to bring claims but rarely did so, as the law adopted very different standards when judging their claims and never awarded the large sums of money that women were able to obtain.

1

To reflect this, throughout the book I have used pronouns which represent a woman bringing a breach of promise claim and a man defending it. The few claims brought by men against women are covered in their own chapter.

This study of breach of promise between 1780 and 1970 focusses on the social history of the claim rather than its legal development and I have consciously simplified discussion of the law and legal structures. The cases included here have been chosen for the social aspects they represent. In selecting examples I have endeavoured to illustrate the wider picture and when using cases that seem unique I have indicated this. I have also been very sparing in the use of examples after 1930, as by that time the claim was becoming relatively unusual. People who have been involved in breach of promise claims are still alive and I have no wish cause any hurt or distress.

Some of my source material has been drawn from contemporary newspapers, which provide fascinating insights but can also be tantalisingly brief. Full names, ages, occupations and places of residence for plaintiff and defendant are often not available. Lack of detail also makes it very hard to discover what happened to many women after their breach of promise hearing, and in some cases there is no way of knowing whether a name in the records relates to the plaintiff. In this respect women with more unusual names are an asset.

I entered details of the breach of promise claims into a database. The statistics included in this study are drawn from that information. For those with an interest in this side of my work, further analysis is provided in Appendix 2.

In the year spent researching and writing this book I have enjoyed support and practical assistance from a number of people, some of whom are unknown to me. Thanks are expressed to anyone who has been involved in digitising material for use on-line. To have located the range of information I have discovered from microfilm would have been impossible and I feel this study is an example of how the easier searchability of source material will, in the coming years, lead to a deeper understanding of some hidden aspects of history.

My editor, Jen Newby, displayed immediate enthusiasm when I

first mentioned breach of promise and encouraged me to develop an editorial proposal whilst I was still considering whether the topic would yield sufficient material to sustain a book. She has since been a fount of wisdom and constructive challenge as my research led me away from what we initially thought the book would be about and into new and unexpected discoveries.

I would also like to thank Rachel Anchor, Mark Stevens, and Broadmoor Hospital, who have all provided assistance with individual queries. The staff of the Local Studies Library in Ashton-under-Lyne have offered practical support and shown a genuine interest in the research undertaken in the library. The marriage of Mary Elizabeth Smith was uncovered by Saskia Lettmaier as part of her own research.

My immediate family has been a constant source of support and encouragement and I cannot allow the on-going interest of my husband, sons, daughter-in-law, mother and mother-in-law to pass unnoticed. I am grateful for their tolerance of my time and our conversations being overtaken by numbers of people from literature and history, for assistance with all the aspects of computers and information technology which elude me and for help in sourcing the illustrations used in the book. Other than where credited, illustrations are believed to be out of copyright. Should this not be the case, I will endeavour to correct future editions.

Breach of promise has proved a fascinating study of a legal claim which, like ivy, entwined itself in many aspects of nineteenth century society. Very unusually it is an example of a law where women were more equal than men. To discover how women reacted when they had the whip-hand has been the most unexpected part of the journey.

Denise Bates,
1 September 2013

Chapter 1

Discrimination and Diversities
The Development of Breach of Promise 1780–1815

*Causes of this description were frequently opened with many
observations calculated to inflame jurors' minds and that such
cases called on them to give very large and exemplary damages.*
(*The Times*, **13 December 1800**)

Broken promises of marriage may be as old as the human race.
Boy meets girl, suggests a life-long union and then has second
thoughts. In England, where regulating disputes between
engaged couples was solely the prerogative of the Church Courts
until the seventeenth century, fragmentary records from Chester
Consistory Court show that in 1609, Lucy Lloyd complained that
John Whitbie had failed to marry her at Michaelmas. In 1621,
Margaret Hollinshead reported that Thomas Orwell of Wilmslow
had breached their matrimonial contract and offered her £10 not
to bring a charge against him. In 1662, James Urmston set out his
reasons for not marrying Hester Griffin and at Salisbury during
1667, John Aubrey began a three-year dispute with Joan Sumner
who had jilted him. Between 1703 and 1754, the Consistory Court
for London received a few complaints about broken engagements,
and many more about adulterous spouses. Unfortunately, the
outcomes of these early disputes remain a tantalising mystery.

Marriage was regarded as a religious state rather than a civil
contract and representatives of the Church of England were
empowered to decide what action to take when an affianced man
or woman refused to go through with their marriage ceremony.
Whether the jilted person had a remedy depended on how the
engagement had been formed. If the engagement was a betrothal
it was agreed in the present tense, with words such as 'you are
my spouse'. This created a binding contract and the couple could

be ordered by the Church Court to take their marriage vows. A betrothal was often seen as a safeguard when the marriage was designed to increase family wealth, power or prestige. It would have been equally attractive to impetuous young lovers fearing parental opposition to their union because, as soon as the words had been spoken, neither party was free to marry anyone else. If an engagement was declared in the future tense, using words such as 'you will be my spouse', the contract was not seen as binding and the Church Courts could not compel the couple to wed, unless they had cohabited.

The power of clergymen to deal with broken engagements ended abruptly on 24 March 1754. The next day, 'An Act for the better preventing of clandestine Marriages', more commonly known as Lord Hardwicke's Marriage Act, came into effect. The new regulations were designed to eradicate the problems caused by irregular marriages which, by 1750, were considered a threat to law-abiding society. Although the Church of England already had sensible procedures and formalities about giving public notice of an intended marriage and ensuring that both parties were competent to marry, these could be ignored with impunity. If the ceremony was conducted by a Church of England priest then the marriage was considered to be legal whether it took place in a church, a public house or a prison; whether banns had been called or not and irrespective of the ages of the couple.

Hardwicke's Act decreed that a marriage would only be valid if it was performed in a church, after the calling of banns and with the consent of a parent or guardian for anyone under 21, other than a widow or widower. To forestall any attempts to circumvent the new law, the Act absolutely abolished the right of the Church Courts to enforce engagements made in the present or future tense, 'any law or usage to the contrary notwithstanding'. The only redress a jilted person had against a recalcitrant fiancé was to bring a claim against them in the civil court.

Financial claims arising from broken engagements, though rare, had been dealt with by the civil courts from the seventeenth century as breaches of contract. Unlike the Church, where persuasion, or the threat of excommunication, could be used to coerce a hesitant party to the altar, civil courts had no power, or wish, to compel an unwilling person to marry. The only claim a complainant (known in legal terms as a plaintiff) could make was for damages.

The main sources of detailed information about breach of promise claims in the civil courts are newspaper reports. Although it is unlikely that all cases were noticed by the press, from 1787, enough reports have survived in newspaper archives to allow tentative conclusions to be drawn. Sadly, some cases were recorded with tantalising brevity. The only surviving information about one high profile claim in 1788 is that 'a lady' sued 'a gentleman' for £10,000 and was awarded £600. Other cases, perhaps more interesting because they included an unusual feature or scandalous detail, were reported in slightly greater depth. In July 1793, a 60-year-old man arrived at a Bedford church with a different bride, whilst the woman who had expected to marry him that day watched in disbelief. She was awarded £50. A month later, 40-year-old Miss Ellis, who forgot to mention her brood of illegitimate children to a 22-year-old farmer's son, lost her claim for damages at Chester Assizes, the jury believing that she had tricked the naïve young man into making a secret proposal.

Following Hardwicke's Act, a specific claim for breach of promise of marriage gradually developed in the civil courts and became the accepted way to resolve any problem associated with a failed engagement. In trying to broker fair and reasonable solutions for individual plaintiffs and defendants, jury decisions appear to have drifted from strict principles of contract law and began to include an element of moral judgement about the conduct of the two parties in the claim. In 1803, whilst presiding over the case of Leeds v Cook, Lord Ellenborough told the jury that 'this species of action has more shades of discrimination and greater diversities than perhaps any other action whatever'.

By 1803, damages in breach of promise claims were no longer calculated in the same way as in other breaches of contract. They drifted towards another branch of law, known as tort, which dealt with claims when a plaintiff had suffered some harm, not necessarily physical. Tort law was more generous than contract law and allowed a plaintiff to obtain compensation for the injury inflicted by the defendant, over and above any other losses sustained. As well as the financial value of the lost marriage, most plaintiffs received an additional amount for hurt feelings. Precisely how and when this occurred is not known but it is perhaps not surprising that it did. At the end of the eighteenth century, two common claims in tort law arose from sexual relationships between men and women. Men could be sued for damages for seduction if they made a girl pregnant and then refused to marry her. Damages included a sum for the loss of her reputation, in addition to any financial costs her parent might incur because of the pregnancy. A man whose wife had committed adultery could sue her lover for criminal conversation, often demanding, and sometimes receiving, exemplary damages. In both of these situations, the defendant had behaved dishonourably and deserved to be punished through his pocket.

It would not have been a great leap of reasoning for respectable members of a society that placed high value on honourable behaviour, to treat a broken promise of marriage as conduct that sometimes warranted exemplary damages, whether or not there had been a sexual relationship between the couple. This served a dual purpose: to make a proper recompense to the injured party and to convey the disapproval of polite society towards ungentlemanly conduct. It would have seemed especially desirable when a young woman was upset about her broken engagement but could not easily identify what she had lost in financial terms.

By the time Lord Ellenborough spoke of the complexity of the claim for breach of promise, a number of different strands had come to feature in these cases, in addition to recovering out-of-pocket expenses. These various aspects are illustrated clearly by three cases heard between 1787 and 1803. In February 1787, a young army lieutenant, Charles Bourne, sued a rich, elderly widow, Maria de Comerford. Lawyers for both parties stressed that it was not uncommon for females to bring an action for breach of promise, but 'rather singular' for a man to do so. Not mentioned by either barrister, or the judge, was the size of Bourne's claim: £20,000. This appears to have included £10,000 which Maria had promised to settle on him and £2,000 towards his debts. Lack of comment by barristers or the press about the size of the claim, or its individual elements, indicates that such sums were not out of the ordinary.

When the judge, Lord Loughborough, summed up the case for the jury he emphasised that a definite offer and acceptance, which are intrinsic elements of forming a valid contract, applied to claims for breach of promise. He also stressed that in a contract as serious as matrimony, a promise of marriage should not be inferred from levity of expression or levity of conduct. It was not necessary to accept in writing or to use particular words but acceptance of the offer must be explicit.

It seems probable that either Bourne's offer or Maria's acceptance did not meet the standard then required to bring a contract into existence as Loughborough appears to have been steering the jury towards a verdict for Maria, on the grounds that there was no contract to be broken. Despite the hints, the jury decided that a contract had been made and that the lieutenant had been jilted. They awarded him a shilling in damages, a very low sum but one that forced Maria, as the loser, to pay Bourne's legal costs as well as her own. Press comment suggests that the jury had wanted to avoid the young officer being declared responsible for settling the legal bills of a wealthy woman who had behaved foolishly.

Although decisions made by juries did not form binding precedents, effective lawyers influenced the judgement of jurors by revealing similar claims where the jury had decided a debatable point in a particular way, yet without disclosing the full circumstances. Barristers such as Thomas Erskine and William Garrow, who were active in the courts of the time, gained reputations for arguing forcefully and ingeniously on behalf of their clients, playing on the emotions of the jurors as they did so. Humane juries appear to have assisted breach of promise claims to escape the strict requirements of contract law because they occasionally ignored the facts in order to achieve what they considered was a reasonable outcome for both parties.

By 1800, breach of promise claims involving middle-class and respectable working-class women usually emphasised the grievous nature of the emotional injury to the young woman and her blighted prospects in life. It was considered very unlikely that a woman who had been courted and then abandoned would receive another offer of marriage; unless her honour and reputation were vindicated in public. These sentiments, which feature in several claims as the eighteenth century drew to a close, were given full expression in the case of Andrews v Morrison in 1801, when a tradesman's daughter sued a London tradesman. Her barrister, Thomas Erskine, the son of an Earl and himself a Member of Parliament, waxed lyrical on the theme of hurt feelings in a speech which must have taken ten minutes to deliver. The following extract from newspaper coverage gives a flavour of his oration:

> *If there was any case that more deserved attention than another, it was that which involved the consideration of an injury done to a woman. It did not require many words to convey an idea of the irreparable injury sustained by a female who was disappointed in her marriage with a man whose assiduities had gained her affections. Let her be as beautiful as Diana and as accomplished as possible she could never appear as she was before she became the object of such an insult. She had not the same chance of securing another marriage. Men were actuated by a sense of pride, which made them averse to marrying a woman another might have had if he had thought fit. There was no smoke without fire, and if the reason was not given in public a man would wonder why another man had rejected her and whether there was any blame on her part.*

Erskine's emotional pleading netted £200 to avenge Miss Andrews' broken reputation and soothe her wounded spirit. This was an average award of damages at that time and would have reflected what a tradesman could afford to pay. The honours of Elizabeth Jones and Miss Southerton, probably middle-class women with wealthy suitors, had also recently been avenged with awards of a thousand pounds or more.

Upper-class lawyers regularly argued, with apparent sincerity, that a refined woman whose spirit had been wounded by a false lover deserved exemplary recompense for her broken heart. Meanwhile working-class women in the burgeoning industrial towns were sustaining irreparable damage to their health from twelve-hour shifts in unregulated factories and coal-mines without anyone suggesting recompense for the serious physical injuries that could blight their lives. As Erskine explained, 'a man or woman might bear much, but a wounded spirit, who could bear?'

Refined women did not have a monopoly on breach of promise claims, but those brought by women who earned their own living by manual work were treated differently. A case heard at the Summer

Assizes in York in 1802 was not the first to award damages to a woman whose background could not be claimed as genteel, yet it may be the earliest such case for which a detailed record remains. The courtship could easily feature in the plot of an eighteenth century play.

The plaintiff, Maria Storey, dubbed by her suitor as the 'nymph of the soapsuds', was a laundry maid in the service of Mr Stockdale of Knaresborough in North Yorkshire. Robert Eagle had flirted with her at the out-door wash-tub for a couple of years, making Maria jocular offers of marriage in the hearing of another washerwoman, Mrs Ellen Sly. Maria had consistently rejected them until she heard that Eagle had leased a pub and was now a man with prospects. By this time Eagle had impulsively proposed to a 'd----d woman' in nearby Harrogate. It is unclear whether he proposed again to Maria after this, but when she unexpectedly agreed to marry him Eagle decided to try to extricate himself from the engagement to the 'd----d woman'. She immediately threatened to sue for breach of promise, pointing out that she had two witnesses to his proposal. Eagle reluctantly married her and was told by Ellen Sly that he ought to give Maria £30 in compensation. The case ended up in court and the jury awarded Maria £50, a twelfth of Eagle's capital.

In arguing Maria's case, the lawyers placed scant emphasis on any emotional harm she had suffered and considered that as she still had her employment there was little to compensate her for. The sum awarded to Maria was low in comparison with awards to women who did not earn their own living and appears to have exceeded £30 only because Eagle himself felt this was insufficient. Breach of promise claims may have been available to women of all social classes but there are indications of class distinction and value judgement in the way they were conducted and decided.

Maria's case demonstrates that the claim for breach of promise, and the likely damages, were well-known amongst the working classes. After Hardwicke's Act deprived the Church Courts of their power to enforce marriage when a couple had cohabited, poor women who were seduced and then abandoned with an illegitimate child turned to breach of promise with varying degrees of success. Sarah Heydon, although pregnant, lost her claim in 1789 because she had refused Mr Hutching's proposal and he chose not to renew it.

Seduction and illegitimacy as elements of a breach of promise claim do not feature in the extant newspaper reports of eighteenth century breach of promise cases involving more genteel women. If pregnancy was involved then middle-class parents brought a claim for seduction instead. The person entitled in law to a seduced woman's services, usually one of her parents, could claim compensation from the seducer if her pregnancy involved them in expense or left them to maintain a daughter who was unlikely to find a husband. In April 1802, Theodosia Barritt won £1,000 for the seduction and pregnancy of her 18-year-old daughter, Maria. This was an exceptionally large award and appears to have been made because Maria's wealthy fiancé, Mr Hollamby, abandoned her after an assault that would now be described as date-rape. As Maria's engagement was public knowledge she would have won substantial damages for breach of promise had she brought a claim, which suggests that the middle-classes at that point did not use breach of promise in cases of seduction. The position may have changed early in 1803.

In March 1803, *The Observer* published an anonymous epigram, 'A Breach of Promise the strongest proof of – Breeding', hinting at the link between pregnancy and breach of promise.

Clarinda promises to visit soon
Indeed, she's only waiting for a moon.
Four following moons have since their progress run.
And now Clarinda's waiting for – a son.

The earliest successful breach of promise case involving an illegitimate child born to a genteel woman to be noted by the press may have been heard in March 1805. Elizabeth Forster, the daughter of a respectable Warwickshire farmer, claimed damages from Mr Hoblin, a neighbouring farmer. They had been engaged for two years, but when she became pregnant he refused to marry her. She was awarded £400 damages, one fifth of his capital. There is no indication that her father exercised his right to sue for seduction.

The extension of the scope of breach of promise law to cover seduction is an interesting development in women's rights and it is logical that it may have originated with working-class women who were more likely to have left the family home to earn a living. Once away from home a woman was no longer providing any services to her parents so they could not obtain damages for seduction, depriving her of any right to compensation. A breach of promise claim closed this loophole and gave a woman a remedy in her own right if she surrendered her virtue to her fiancé. Any damages awarded belonged to her to spend as she chose. Used wisely they could provide her and the child with a degree of independence or security.

Breach of promise claims were not available to all unwed mothers. If an engagement had been announced, or a ring or marriage licence procured, then a woman would succeed in a claim. Those who succumbed to words whispered to effect the seduction were in a precarious position, as without a witness it was impossible to prove that marriage had been offered. Even if they could prove the promise, a contract made to secure sexual favours could not be enforced as it was deemed immoral. The rights of a seduced woman were limited to an order from the parish obliging the father of her child to pay for her confinement, which cost around £2, and to maintain the child at the rate set by the parish, until it was 12 years old.

Claims for breach of promise and for seduction ran in parallel for several decades. From the evidence available it seems that a woman who could prove breach of promise took that route because of the likelihood of higher damages being awarded. In 1818, when Elizabeth Elliott's father sued Joseph Nicklin, his daughter's former fiancé, for seduction, the defence lawyer contended that when an engagement had been broken, a woman should claim for breach of promise rather than her father being rewarded for her disgrace. This ingenious reasoning was intended to allow 19-year-old Nicklin to avoid paying any compensation, as he was too young to be held to account for his false promise. The appalled jurors refused to allow the brash youth to walk away from the consequences of his duplicity and awarded Mr Elliott £1,000, to support his daughter and grandson.

Later that year, Sarah Settle, the mother of an illegitimate child, was awarded £700 damages for breach of promise after John Crumbleholme, the father of her child, married another woman. In 1819, her mother received £200 for Sarah's seduction in a separate claim. This does not appear to have set a precedent for a woman and her parent both receiving substantial compensation for a pregnancy and the claim for seduction gradually became a claim of last resort for the families of women who were unable to prove a broken promise of marriage. When summing up seduction cases, some judges indicated whether the woman would be able to prove breach of promise and juries seem to have taken this into account when assessing damages, giving good awards in deserving cases if a woman was unable to prove that a promise to marry had been made.

***

Whilst a variety of social developments were turning breach of promise into a complex form of court action, a spinster with acute powers of social observation was penning some of England's most enduring fiction. Jane Austen's novels capture the middle-class and respectable working-class background to which the majority of breach of promise plaintiffs belonged. Austen wrote about a world she knew well, chronicling the trials and tribulations that could befall a young lady treading the path to marriage; 'the only honourable provision for well-educated young women of small fortune, and however uncertain of giving happiness, must be their pleasantest preservative from want'.

This threat of penury stalked the daughters of middle-class gentlemen. In *Pride and Prejudice*, Mr Bennett's estate is to be inherited by a male cousin. After covering the family's living costs from his income he is unable to set aside sufficient money to provide his five daughters with a marriage settlement which would guarantee them a respectable husband. Their future fortune is just £800 each after the death of their mother. Invested in a secure manner at a three per cent return, this would yield an income of £24 a year. In contrast, wealthy tradesman's daughters such as the Bingley sisters inherited capital of £20,000, which would have yielded £600 a year. This made them attractive if they chose to enter the marriage market, but prevented them from being obliged to do so, or to accept, like Charlotte Lucas, a marriage of convenience when an unexpected opportunity

14

belatedly presented itself in the form of pompous clergyman, William Collins, heir to Mr Bennett's estate.

Few options were open to well-bred young women in straitened circumstances. For most, being a wife with her own household, even in a loveless marriage, was preferable to a grudging home with relatives, perhaps expected to act as an unpaid servant in return for her keep until she died. Gainful employment outside the home was not plentiful. A post as a governess or companion made use of a woman's skills and accomplishments, providing a roof over her head and a salary of around £20 a year. It also enabled her friends to pity her misfortune, rather than being embarrassed by her poverty. Women who were exceptionally skilled with a needle could earn some income from dressmaking, helping them to pay their own way in someone else's home. Working-class women had a variety of ways to earn a living, in factories, coal mines, hostelries and domestic service. These jobs usually involved very physical work and, irrespective of any notions of taste, it is unlikely that women who had been brought up as ladies would have had the strength or stamina to cope with manual employment.

Marriage was a commercial contract to which both the bride and the groom were expected to contribute resources. A man brought his existing capital and his future expectations, which could be an assured inheritance or an assured salary from an occupation or profession. Heiresses such as Louisa and Caroline Bingley brought a large capital sum in their own right. Most women relied on their father to be able to pay capital into their marriage settlement and the more daughters he had the less he could do for any of them. As married women were not allowed to own property until 1883, it was conventional for a parent to channel his gift towards the couple's future into a settlement. This was a trust fund set up to protect the woman's assets by preventing her husband from deciding how any money given by her father should be invested or spent. Before the wedding took place a woman transferred any property she owned into her settlement to stop it falling under her husband's control. The bridegroom usually added a capital sum to the trust to provide for her future widowhood. All funds, whatever their source, were managed for the woman's benefit by trustees, who dealt with the income from investments on terms that had been agreed in writing by the husband-to-be before the marriage took place.

Negotiating a marriage settlement could be a complicated business and included several parties. The bridegroom's father might be involved if he was providing any capital on his son's behalf. Fathers of grooms could drive a hard bargain, requiring a substantial contribution from the bride's family in return for their own. Arranged marriages without choice were not the norm, but romantic love between the couple was not considered important until the mid-nineteenth century. The son of a wealthy man was often expected to marry a woman who would bring yet more wealth into the family, rather than one who had little to contribute. One practical factor that smoothed the way for Jane and Elizabeth Bennett to marry rich husbands, despite their own limited expectations, was the good fortune that Charles Bingley and Fitzwilliam Darcy had both lost their parents before meeting their future wives and risked no parental displeasure by choosing to marry for love. Wills disinheriting a wealthy man who fell in love with a woman his family did not approve of were written by solicitors and were not works of fiction.

Jane Austen did not use breach of promise in her novels, but during her lifetime a number of court cases were reported in various newspapers and she must have been aware of the claim and of its potential impact on those entering the marriage stakes. In order to drive her main plots Austen included such risque topics as duelling, seduction, illegitimacy and elopement by her supporting cast. The absence of breach of promise in her novels may suggest that by 1810 it was already considered a mercenary and vulgar action.

Despite not dealing with the subject directly, the potential for a breach of promise claim to ruin a man lurks within *Sense and Sensibility*. As a naïve adolescent, Edward Ferrars formed an unwise and secret engagement with pretty, mercenary Lucy Steele. Although he realised his mistake, Ferrars chose to remain loyal to her. Honour is the reason ascribed to his reluctant constancy, but at a time when damages were soaring, the calculating Miss Steele would have sued for substantial compensation for her lost marriage and ruined any hopes Ferrars might have entertained of ever supporting himself decently, much less providing for a wife.

Much remains hidden about the formative period of breach of promise claims after the Church lost its right to decree that a wedding should take place. Early claims appear to have related to poor women trying to obtain support for an illegitimate child, to richer ones recovering money paid to the person who broke the engagement and to men recovering the costs of preparing a home when a woman refused to marry.

Within a generation, women had begun to claim and receive compensation for the lifestyle they had lost when jilted and for insult to their reputation. Information gleaned from newspapers and contemporary fiction suggests that this aspect of the claim was regarded with distaste and those who publicly sued for damages above and beyond any losses they could quantify may have been considered lacking in decorum. By 1815, as 20 years of war in Europe drew to a welcome close, the many diversities of a claim for breach of promise were poised to reveal themselves to a wider audience.

Chapter 2

ARTFUL AND ABANDONED HUSSIES
THE HEYDAY OF BREACH OF PROMISE 1816–1869

First love was the strongest, and perhaps the only
love a woman felt.
(*The Observer*, **23 February 1835**)

For almost a generation, newspapers had been filled with descriptions of the horrors of the French Revolution and the successive battles of the Napoleonic wars. With the final defeat of Napoleon Bonaparte at Waterloo in 1815, the content of newspapers altered perceptibly as military news became less significant, releasing space for other stories. Editors began to fill their empty columns with reports from the law-courts, covering routine work rather than just the high-profile or particularly interesting cases.

Some of the breach of promise cases heard at this time reveal that claims were brought against upper-class men by plaintiffs who were their social inferiors. In 1816, governess Anne Lancey, the daughter of a mathematics tutor at Greenwich Naval College, was awarded £1,500 from her wealthy former employer. Robert Hunter had proposed to her after the death of his wife but a few months later he abruptly ended the engagement without giving any reason. Anne's family believed that her comparatively lowly station in life had led Hunter to reconsider his offer. The same year, to popular approval, a grocer's sister, Ann Matchiff, received £1,500 from a Leicestershire baronet, Sir Willoughby Dixie, at Derby Assizes when she proved that he had proposed to her many years before.

Newspaper reports started to provide much more detail about breach of promise cases but this information has to be treated with caution. It is unwise to take any claims by lawyers or journalists about the conduct, motivation or wealth of either party at face value. The case of 22-year-old barmaid Maria Spenser and 29-year-old attorney, William Cole, heard in London in 1819, demonstrates how lawyers selected facts to place their client in the best light possible and to malign the other party, as well as how journalists and editors sometimes adopted a less than objective stance when covering a case.

A concise report in *The Times* portrays Maria, a country girl visiting her married sister, as a poor but highly principled and modest young woman who was prevailed upon to vindicate her character, and that of her publican brother-in-law, Henry Reynolds, when Cole accused them of having an affair in the hearing of others. *The Observer* gave a more detailed account of the trial and revealed that the slanderous comment was in fact made in private to Reynolds, who then publicised Cole's drunken words by repeating them to anyone who would listen. Maria refused to accept the apology Cole had later made or to negotiate damages in a private settlement and instead chose to take her case before a jury, who awarded her £500.

The partisan selection of the evidence, initially by the barristers and then by newspapers, makes it impossible to decide whether Maria was very high-minded or just a grasping young woman. At that time, neither a plaintiff nor a defendant was allowed to give evidence about their case and it was unusual for a woman to attend court to observe proceedings. The fact that Maria was sitting prominently behind her lawyers, perhaps adds weight to the view that she was less modest than she had been portrayed by her legal team.

The number of breach of promise cases increased in the early 1820s and there appear to have been 50 per cent more claims reaching court between 1821 and 1825 than in the previous five years between 1816 and 1820. In December 1827, the judge about to preside over the claim of Martha Scott against William Wickenden, remarked to the lawyers in court that 'this sort of complaint' seemed to be on the increase. The defence barrister immediately responded that the verdicts and damages given in breach of promise cases provided an incentive for them to be brought.

Two factors account for the increase in claims: a success rate of almost 100 per cent for female plaintiffs and the liberality of juries in compensating them. Levels of damages had been rising since 1805, and in April 1818, a Lancaster jury awarded Mary Alice Orford a record £7,000. Between 1816 and 1825 only seven of the 54 awards were less than £100 and the most frequent sum awarded was £500. Eight women received £1,000 or more.

This high success rate in breach of promise cases occurred because the claim drifted further and further away from the law of contract. In 1826, formal acceptance of the offer of marriage by the bride-to-be was explicitly dispensed with by the Chief Justice, Sir William Best. Eighteen-year-old Charlotte Daniel sat in silence as her mother told Charles Bowles that Charlotte's father had made no objection to his proposal. In court, Bowles's lawyers argued that Charlotte's failure to give her own assent meant that there was no contract for Bowles to breach. The Chief Justice immediately dismissed the argument by ruling that Charlotte's lack of objection to the proposal represented valid acceptance of Bowles' offer.

The circumstances of this case may explain why the Chief Justice ruled as he did. Bowles was 45 when he met Charlotte in Italy and his proposal to her parents was part of a deliberate strategy to seduce her. Shortly afterwards the pair eloped and returned to London, where they lived as man and wife. Charlotte's parents then discovered that Bowles was already married. By the time Charlotte was located by her family she was pregnant. She returned to Italy to give birth, which meant that it was not possible under English law to compel Bowles to maintain the child. Chief Justice Best was clearly angry that an army officer had behaved in a dishonourable manner, abusing the hospitality of a brother officer to seduce his daughter, and may have ruled on the question of acceptance in this manner to ensure that Bowles had to pay damages. The jury awarded Charlotte £1,500, a substantial recompense. At that time it was possibly the largest award made against a man who was not extremely wealthy.

Defeating a claim became almost impossible in the 1820s, even for men with apparently strong defences. In 1823, Susannah Horne was awarded £2 damages from prosperous James Miller at the Norfolk Assizes, in a verdict that seems designed to ensure that, as the loser, Miller would have to pay impoverished Susannah's legal costs. Miller's barrister voiced strong doubts about whether there was a valid proposal, as contract law required an engagement to be formed in a serious and considered manner, but the only occasion when Miller mentioned marriage had been when both he and Susannah were intoxicated. After the alleged proposal, Susannah spent some time in jail, where it became obvious to the authorities that she was pregnant and the local magistrates ordered her to name the father so that he could be forced to maintain the child. Susannah tried to foist paternity on a number of her lovers, which should have allowed Miller to plead that Susannah's immoral conduct with other men entitled him to break any promise of marriage.

Claims of dubious integrity and those where the woman had sustained no discernible harm were routinely taken to court, usually obtaining damages out of all proportion to any injury. Solicitors and their staff were particularly adept at identifying when a member of their own families had a claim, and some appear to have plotted to entrap unsuspecting men. In 1825, Caroline Elkington, the 18-year-old daughter of a Birmingham solicitor, was sent to stay in London with her brother, who was also a lawyer. She was introduced to a young surgeon, Mr Copeland, and after a brief acquaintance he proposed. A few months later, Copeland decided not to marry as, on more mature reflection, he realised that he could not afford to support Caroline in a suitable level of comfort. Her father immediately stated a claim for damages.

As the case progressed, the defence lawyers revealed that a separate breach of promise claim was being pursued on behalf of Caroline's elder sister, who had also spent time living unchaperoned in London with her brother. Yet another claim had been instigated against the man who introduced Caroline to Copeland, though the grounds were not specified. Caroline was awarded £250. There is no record of her sister's claim, suggesting that the other defendant came to a private arrangement. An award of £250 would have been a strong incentive to a man of modest means not to risk facing a jury.

Behind every successful plaintiff was a legal team. The 1820s saw a rapid increase in litigation, as men of the law realised that claims for damages provided a way to make a profitable living. The high success rate in breach of promise claims attracted legal professionals like a magnet and there were reports of solicitors visiting neighbourhoods, tracing women who had experienced a disappointment in love and advising them whether they had a case. When a claim was made, another solicitor then obtained business from a defendant who needed legal advice. If the case came to court, each party would need to engage a barrister to argue on their behalf, resulting in more costs for the loser.

By the end of the decade, claims where the woman had suffered no appreciable harm were derided as 'attorney's actions', brought for no reason except to enable to a solicitor to claim his fees. Some solicitors began to take strong cases on a no-win-no-fee basis. So long as the case succeeded, the solicitor's costs were paid by the defendant. What damages the woman received was immaterial. The growth of the attorney's action in the 1820s can be discerned in an increased number of claims from lower-class women, a fall in the level of damages towards the end of the decade, and occasional derisory awards; though a defendant could not depend on this.

In 1828, Sally Simpson, a 58-year-old smallholder from Cumberland, had allegedly been told by an attorney that a jocular offer of marriage made 19 years earlier by 62-year-old landowner, Joseph Timperton, entitled her to compensation when he married someone else. The judge displayed no doubt that Timperton's bantering comments had formed a binding proposal and, to the surprise of the spectators at the Lancaster Assizes, who were expecting very small damages, the jury awarded Sally £350.

Declining standards of evidence and elevated levels of compensation in the 1820s were not confined to female plaintiffs in breach of promise cases. The early part of the decade was the only time when jilted men could obtain anything more than trivial damages. A very low standard of evidence was accepted at Burnley in 1823, when Thomas Whittam claimed £1,000 damages from his 55-year-old cousin, Mr Smith, for the seduction of his 17-year-old daughter, Janet. Smith denied the allegation and pointed out that at the time the teenager became pregnant, 19-year-old Thomas Jackson was staying with the family and sleeping in the adjoining bedroom to Janet's. The baby must have been born several weeks prematurely if she had conceived on the date she stated in court. Despite all the indications that Smith was being set up by the Whittam family, the jury awarded £100 damages against him.

Around 1820, damages in seduction cases jumped from less

than £100 to a few hundred. In Janet Whittam's case, the jury may have heeded the request of the defence barrister that 'if they felt bound to give a verdict for the plaintiff, they would, under the circumstances, give only nominal damages'. Implicitly accepting the word of a woman, however implausible, appears to have been a matter of chivalry at that time.

After 1828, the number of breach of promise cases reported by the press started to decline as a number of other major issues emerged to fill newspaper columns for almost two decades. There was the controversy of Catholic Emancipation, followed by three years of agitation for Parliamentary Reform and the eventual passing of the Great Reform Bill of 1832. There were four general elections in the 1830s. Slavery was abolished in the British Colonies in 1833. After several years of campaigning and two shocking investigations, a Factories Act was passed in 1834 to curb the exploitation of children and young people in the textile industry and a further act passed in 1844 extended some protection to adult women and to other industries. King William IV died and an 18-year-old girl became Queen. A draconian and unpopular system for relief of the poor was introduced. The Chartists, an umbrella movement of working men, began to agitate for further political reform, whilst the Anti-Corn Law League of manufacturers and entrepreneurs campaigned for the removal of tariffs and duties, which they felt were harming the country's economic prospects. A severe famine affected Ireland and ultimately led to the repeal of the Corn Laws in 1846, and the break-up of the Tory Party after its leader, Sir Robert Peel put national imperatives above party loyalties.

Against these high profile stories there was less space in newspapers for breach of promise cases, unless there was something particularly newsworthy about them, or a short paragraph to fill. A number of the cases reported in this period had features which would either have amused or shocked readers.

With hindsight, the most influential breach of promise case ever heard came to public attention in March 1837. The irony of Bardell v Pickwick is that it was a fictional case; a satire penned by the young Charles Dickens, who used it to illustrate what he saw as a legal system corrupted by the greed and self-interest of lawyers. Its influence persisted throughout the nineteenth century and possibly shaped the laws of evidence in breach of promise claims in a way that Dickens could never have intended: by helping to reduce standards even further. In *Oliver Twist* (1837), Dickens had one of his characters observe that 'the law is an ass'. If he, a layman, did inadvertently assist a further relaxation in standards of evidence, then his observation was very accurate.

It is sometimes difficult for the modern mind to grasp precisely how influential the views of a respected individual could be in the nineteenth century. By 1850, the renown of the novelist was such that Mr Justice Maule referred to *The Pickwick Papers* whilst summing up the evidence in a debt case for the jury, stating that, 'he, (the learned judge) did not mean that the jury should look upon that work as an authority like the various law reports, but he thought they might safely take it for granted that where that author mentioned any practice as being of common occurrence in London he was generally pretty near the mark'.

Dickens worked in a solicitor's office before he became a journalist and spent hours in the London law-courts reporting on the various cases heard. He realised that breach of promise claims, along with many others, were serving corrupt lawyers and grasping plaintiffs perhaps more than they served justice and his novels routinely portrayed lawyers as disreputable. *The Pickwick Papers* was no exception. Published as a monthly serial it comprised a loosely-linked set of comical adventures involving a group of male friends. The hugely popular instalment published in March 1837 featured the trial of the amiable and elderly Samuel Pickwick, who was being sued by his middle-aged, widowed landlady, Martha Bardell, for breach of promise.

The alleged breach arose from a misunderstanding on Martha's part. Pickwick clumsily enquired whether his landlady could accommodate his new servant and she interpreted his words that two could live as cheaply as one, for a proposal. When, in all innocence, Pickwick never again referred to marriage or set a wedding date she consulted lawyers who took the case 'on spec', confident that they could win their fee by loading Pickwick's words with a meaning they had never held.

Not all breach of promise trials were noted in the press, and it is possible that the author had observed a situation similar to the dramatic scenario he described, but it seems more likely that the author carefully constructed Samuel Pickwick's predicament for dramatic effect, stretching the limits of a breach of promise claim as he did so. The case contained several unusual factors: a couple about whom there had been no suspicion of an attachment; a situation in which innocent words took on an ambiguous meaning; a surprised woman who unexpectedly fainted into Pickwick's arms and the almost simultaneous arrival of three witnesses, his best friends, who mistook this for an embrace. A convenient series of incidents was not a normal feature in breach of promise claims.

Bardell v Pickwick has been treated as evidence that inferred proposals were an established feature of breach of promise cases in the 1830s. Prior to March 1837, nothing has been found to suggest that even the most devious lawyers had argued that an engagement could arise without an unambiguous offer of marriage being made by the defendant. Inferring an engagement from the conduct of the parties was a significant development of the breach of promise claim. It would have been widely reported in the press and the jury's verdict would likely have been the subject of an appeal.

The first mention in the British press of the concept that an engagement could arise without a formal proposal was in the summer of 1838. *The Guardian* and *The Observer* both reported that a judge in Vermont, USA, had ruled that no explicit promise was needed to create a marriage contract. Long-continued attention or intimacy with a female would suffice. *The Observer* considered that the judge's ruling was curious. If a development abroad was noticed and commented on by two newspapers in this manner, then it seems unlikely that it was a feature of English law at that point.

It was not long before inferred engagements became part of breach of promise law in England. In June 1839, Elizabeth Irwin claimed damages from recently-married Reverend Luxmore, the vicar of Barnstaple. For evidence of the proposal, Elizabeth relied on letters Luxmore had written more than a decade ago, sent whilst she was visiting Europe. The judge pointed out to the jury that the letters contained no reference to marriage, but rather than ruling that Elizabeth had not proved an engagement, he left the jurors to decide whether they felt able to infer Luxmore's intention to marry from the correspondence. The jurors, possibly more aware of the case of Bardell v Pickwick, than legal decisions in Vermont, decided that they could, and awarded the fortunate spinster £400.

Between 1821 and 1839, the evidence requirements to prove a broken promise of marriage disintegrated with a caprice that is difficult to comprehend. Born out of a wish to help women in difficult circumstances and convey society's disapproval of the bad behaviour of some men, the normal principles of contract law were progressively whittled away. Judges made decisions in the context of specific circumstances, the legal profession then generalised these and its more disreputable members actively connived to take advantage of an increasingly lax claim.

By 1826, it was no longer necessary for a female plaintiff to accept an offer of marriage, so long as she had not positively rejected it. By 1828, an offer did not have to be made in a sober and serious manner, a jocular proposal could be binding. In 1839, when a judge abdicated responsibility for deciding whether a valid offer of marriage had been made, jurors were empowered to infer one from the circumstances of the couple, even when the word marriage had not been uttered by the defendant.

Jurymen played an important role in the decline of standards in breach of promise claims. As the loser of a case was usually ordered to pay the winner's legal costs, juries were prepared to accept very low standards of evidence from a woman when upholding her claim. This made it almost impossible for a man to mount a successful defence, as he was usually richer than the woman, and had probably not behaved as a proper gentleman should, even if he had not offered to marry her. Such well-intentioned chivalry, displaying the humanity of jurors and a belief that a man could afford the damages and legal fees was misguided. It merely entrenched breach of promise claims as a source of enrichment for grasping lawyers and greedy plaintiffs.

The breach of promise claim sank to its most disreputable in the mid-nineteenth century and yielded rich pickings for solicitors who considered their own pockets instead of their client's interests. In 1826, the claim of Miss Etheridge against Mr Croxford, her former employer, was settled by agreement when the judge queried why the defendant's out-of-court offer of £75 and a £25 annuity for their child had been turned down. Croxford's barrister explained that his client had always been prepared to negotiate a settlement, but Miss Etheridge's solicitor had a vested interest in running up his legal fees by taking the case into the court-room. This allegation shows the poor ethics of some solicitors, as the value of what had been rejected was at least £375, far more than Miss Etheridge could have expected from a jury.

Some solicitors touted for clients from the poorer classes, seeking out breaches in which a woman had sustained no harm and persuading her to bring a claim. They were always alert to technical victories that could be won against defendants who had no prospect of paying the damages she obtained. In 1844, the Warwick Assizes awarded £25 to Sarah Bartle, a milliner, against Thomas Roe, a young barber. He was supporting the couple's illegitimate child from his earnings, but had no capital to pay her any damages for breach of promise. Roe's lawyers commented that the only person who would benefit from her claim was the parish attorney who had identified and brought it, as all Sarah was likely to obtain would be an order compelling the defendant to pay her legal bills.

In 1847, Elizabeth Townsend, the daughter of a Gloucester publican, received damages of just one shilling from James Syms, a gentleman's son. Elizabeth, who had recently given birth to his illegitimate child, unwisely settled all her claims against him for £5. She was then contacted by an attorney and told that if she brought a case for breach of promise he could get her £100. After this inducement was revealed in court, the jury stated it had only found in her favour so that Syms would have to pay her legal costs.

Inferred proposals had the potential to provide very rich pickings for lawyers and opportunist plaintiffs but, in practice, many juries exercised restraint. Reverend Luxmore appears unfortunate in having been sued at a time when the concept of an inferred engagement had recently been satirised by Dickens. In 1842, Amelia Rooke asked a jury to infer an engagement on the grounds that elderly Thomas Conway's conduct led her to expect marriage. Conway was 40 years her senior and a first cousin. He explained that any attention he had paid her went no further than courtesy to a young relative. Amelia won the argument, but only a farthing in damages. Jurors were more likely to infer a proposal from the conduct of the parties and award reasonable damages when the woman became pregnant. They were probably right. If a period of courtship was followed by a pregnancy, then it seems very likely that the man had spoken of marriage and that the woman had consented to an intimate relationship on the basis of his promise.

From 1850, the number of claims for breach of promise began to increase markedly. It is not clear why, especially as middle-class women were tending to settle claims by private negotiation rather than asking the jury to decide. As a statement by just one witness, however partisan, could be acceptable proof of a promise to marry, growing laxity in decisions resolving previous cases may have prompted women to pursue their own implausible story.

Finding a witness was a simple matter, and collusion by family or friends was rife. In March 1851, 20-year-old Amelia Harrison, the daughter of an attorney's clerk living in Monmouth, sued William Morgan, a wealthy brewer in his fifties. Through his barrister, Morgan denied the promise, pointing out that Amelia was very friendly with a handsome young excise man, Thomas Hancock, and that the case had been brought to raise some money for them to set up home together. Amelia's witnesses were: her parents, whose identical evidence appeared to have been agreed beforehand; two people who had heard from the Harrison family of a proposal; and a neighbour who, co-incidentally, had been standing within earshot when Morgan allegedly declared his intention to marry Amelia.

In summing up, the judge drew no attention to the glaring weaknesses in the evidence and the jury awarded Amelia £200. The verdict was received with great satisfaction by the 'young folks of Monmouth' who were crowded in the courtroom. Within three months, Amelia had become Mrs Hancock. As Morgan had £10,000 capital, the claim would not have harmed him financially, but the case demonstrates that breach of promise was susceptible to fraud and reveals that judges and jurors were likely to condone this when a young and attractive minx was the perpetrator.

A very similar claim to Amelia Harrison's was heard at Hertford in July 1861, when Anne Hedge, then 19, sued 65-year-old William Barnett. He denied any proposal which, according to her witnesses, had occurred on Gunpowder Plot day in 1858. The only people who knew of the engagement, which had allegedly lasted for almost two years were her relatives. Barnett was a family friend, and may have been chosen for a dupe to raise some money for Anne. In 1860, he received a barrage of solicitor's letters threatening him with a claim for breach of promise unless he came to an arrangement with the lady. During the hearing, a little old man with fiery red hair was identified as Barnett. A loud burst of laughter erupted in the court-room and the judge was observed to be joining in. Barnett lost the case and Anne was awarded £150. By the end of the year Watford marriage records reveal that she had become the wife of another man.

Breach of promise claims were occasionally used to settle other scores. In 1853, wealthy Hannah Hore's claim against George Duke appears to have been brought as part of a wider dispute, as she had no financial need for the £300 damages she obtained. Hannah's family had not wanted her to accept Duke, a much older widower with three children, and tempers on both sides became frayed. Running alongside the breach of promise claim was another case involving slander by Hannah's father against Duke's brother, which was settled by mutual agreement with both parties agreeing to withdraw inflammatory statements about the other side.

Although breach of promise proliferated across society, novelists were no more likely to feature a heroine bringing a claim than their predecessors had been, indicating that popularity did not equate to respectability. Lesser women than Jane Eyre might have sued Edward Rochester for a fortune after he almost succeeded in entrapping her in a bigamous marriage, but Charlotte Bronte's young governess never considered this, finding less shame in begging for a morsel of bread and a night's shelter in an outhouse. *Vanity Fair*, William Thackery's satirical expose of worldly society might have incorporated a plot-line related to breach of promise, but neither amoral Becky Sharp or virtuous Amelia Sedley ever considered this a viable route to wealth or financial security.

Amongst the mid-century novelists, only Anthony Trollope made use of the claim, allowing one of his heroes to be tormented by a grasping and mercenary plaintiff. There was clearly something about breach of promise that implied a woman who brought a claim was no better than she ought to be.

**

The year 1859 provides an unusually detailed snapshot of breach of promise claims. In July 1860, some statistics from the Judicial Returns made to the Home Office about court activity for the previous year were published in *The Times*. These show that a man who wanted to end his engagement could not ignore the risk of a breach of promise claim being made against him. Twenty-two claims, from York to Essex, reached court for a hearing; the tip of an iceberg given that some men would already have come to an arrangement after receiving the court papers, whilst others would have settled after receiving a solicitor's letter.

Twenty-one breach of promise court cases, with varying amounts of detail, have been located in newspapers published in 1859. They are all unremarkable and most are sad or tawdry. One man had continued to court the plaintiff after he married someone else. Another case involved collusion by witnesses. A naval officer realised that his feelings for his fiancée had changed during five years away at sea. One couple had been engaged for 22 years and had a 16-year-old son. A nurse gave up her job and could then only find poorly paid work as a servant when her fiancé changed his mind. One man decided that as both he and his fiancée had hot tempers they were unlikely to live together harmoniously.

All the cases were brought by women. Seventeen cases were won; three were settled by agreement; and one was lost by a plaintiff surprised in bed with another man. All the plaintiffs were lower-middle-class or working-class and five had an illegitimate child. Nine of the couples were from the same social stratum, while in nine others the man was of a higher social standing but only two were significantly so. One woman was of a better social standing and much older and wealthier than her former fiancé. She won her case but received only nominal damages of £5.

The biggest award of damages was £1,000 to a woman abandoned by a rich suitor. There was no child involved and the award was a measure of what she had lost by not becoming a rich man's wife. Reflecting the insubstantial means of working-class defendants, more than half the awards were for £100 or less, with six women receiving just £50. In current values, this is worth approximately £5,000; not a derisory sum but insufficient to maintain a young woman for the rest of her life, even if she invested her capital sensibly. When the distorting effects of the awards of £5 and £1,000 are removed from consideration, then women with children received average damages of £190, whilst the childless obtained £146.

This demonstrates one reason why breach of promise became so popular. Although the claim had developed many disreputable aspects, it had also become the accepted way for a seduced and abandoned woman to extract financial support from her seducer. Between July 1839 and 1869, an illegitimate child featured in 21 per cent of claims. The position of a single mother became very difficult after the Poor Law reforms introduced in 1834 made women wholly responsible for children born out of wedlock. Until 1845, when the law restored to mothers the right to some financial help from the father of their illegitimate child, a breach of promise claim was the only way a woman could obtain any money from him.

The attitude of the press in reporting breach of promise claims probably contributed to the lax approach taken by jurors in the 1850s, who after all, were newspaper readers. Until the 1860s, the press regularly joined in the laughter against defendants who were relieved of a bit of their capital, even if they had been set up by a conniving woman. This demonstrates that jurors were reflecting public opinion when they condoned impudent claims by awarding damages of £100 or more. Ann Hedge's case was widely reported and *The Observer* highlighted it as amusing, describing Barnett as 'a fascinating Lothario'. Marianne Handley, the 19-year-old daughter of a farmer brought a case against a 75-year-old neighbour in 1861, apparently after flirting a proposal out of him. Her counsel declared that if an old man chose to make an old fool of himself, he ought to pay handsomely for it.

Anyone who attempted to obtain money by theft or other forms of deception was liable to a prison sentence with hard labour but entrapping an old man or fabricating a claim for breach of promise against one appears to have been socially acceptable. In 1864, a Mr Ledger named a racehorse Breach of Promise, perhaps an indication that men with money considered the claim risqué but not outrageous.

Within a few years, middle-class tolerance towards breach of promise trials had plummeted. This was probably the result of soaring damages and claims by professional extortioners and promiscuous women. Newspapers adopted the moral high-ground and castigated jurors for their chivalrous impulses towards girls who would have been shown the door as 'artful and abandoned hussies' had they been brought home by a juror's own son. Editors attacked the remnants of an archaic law that prevented breach of promise plaintiffs and defendants from speaking on their own behalf. This was thought to bias the claim in favour of women, as it was difficult for a man to expose lies or collusion by a woman's witnesses. They forgot that amoral men sometimes used a proposal made in private to entice a woman into a sexual relationship and that women failed to win these cases because they could not challenge a defendant's denials of an offer of marriage.

In the 1840s, the ancient law that prevented all plaintiffs and defendants from giving evidence was progressively relaxed, until by 1851, breach of promise and adultery were the only cases where the plaintiff and defendant were not allowed into the witness box. It was thought the temptation to commit perjury would prove too great and, by lying under oath, one of the pair would jeopardise their immortal soul. The position changed in August 1869, when Parliament allowed people involved in breach of promise and adultery cases to choose whether or not to give evidence. The Evidence (Further) Amendment Act heralded a watershed moment for breach of promise. In court, the rules of engagement changed, and the claim gradually swung back towards the law of contract. For the artful and abandoned hussies, the game was over.

Chapter 3

A Substitute for a Shotgun?
The Decline of Breach of Promise 1870–1970

Marriages, I believe, are made in Heaven.
I think I shall wait till I get there.
(William Wilkinson, breach of promise defendant, quoted in
Yorkshire Herald, **8 July 1899)**

Public attitudes towards breach of promise began to change in the 1860s, fuelled by changing values within middle-class society and increasing assertiveness amongst working-class women. By 1870, the middle-classes found that breach of promise claims conflicted with the idealised view of love and marriage they had grown to cherish. This domestic fantasy was sentimentalised by poet, Coventry Patmore, in 1859 when he christened the perfect woman 'the angel in the house', because she uncomplainingly devoted herself to ensuring a comfortable and harmonious home-life for her husband and their children.

As a life of cosy and companionable domesticity was considered most likely to result from a marriage founded on mutual affection and respect, the belief developed that if either of an engaged couple fell out of love, that person should end the engagement and make suitable recompense to the other party, rather than risk a life of wedded misery for them both. By this time, middle-class ladies usually resolved their broken engagements by private negotiation, so there is little evidence of how they behaved when their own hopes of becoming an angel in the house were destroyed. There is no reason to believe that, away from public view, middle-class ladies and their parents disdained to extract substantial financial compensation for a broken heart or damaged reputation.

The new law allowing the plaintiff and defendant to give evidence was not universally welcomed, especially when working-class women sued middle-class men. In 1870, family servant, Polly Frost acquitted herself well under a severe cross-examination of her case and her morals. When the defendant, Josiah Knight, took the witness stand he was inept and confirmed everything Polly had said. Knight's counsel grumbled that the new law was "an act to enable servant girls to compel their master's sons to marry them".

In another case, Annie Jones, a 25-year-old dressmaker, described how her fiancé, Robert Ensor, tricked her into visiting his farm-house where he raped her. After the assault, Ensor gallantly held up a light so that she could repair her torn dress and re-iterated his promise to marry her, if she told no-one what had happened. Three months later, when Annie confirmed that she was pregnant, he ended the engagement saying that her condition was nothing to do with him. He had to pay £200 in damages.

Any apparent advantage to a plaintiff from being able to give evidence proved illusory. The Evidence (Further) Amendment Act 1869 freed women to tell their story from the witness box, but it also stipulated that a successful claim must be supported by proof of an engagement other than the word of the plaintiff. This proof had to be of a 'material standard', a term the Act did not define, but which was intended to eliminate claims based on inference. The need for corroboration made breach of promise a very unusual claim as plaintiffs could win other types of claim on the strength of their own, unsupported testimony. Whilst this might appear an insult to the integrity of women, as they brought the majority of breach of promise claims, female fraudsters had lied about an offer of marriage.

In the 1870s the courts had to decide what was meant by a material standard of corroboration of a promise to marry. Not surprisingly, the issue was raised by defendants looking for a loophole, who began to ask whether the woman's case met the new legal requirements. The task of defining what constituted material evidence fell to three senior judges sitting in the new Court of Appeal, who decided, in 1877, that such evidence could be weak, but it must be direct, and not capable of any meaning other than the defendant's promise to marry the plaintiff. The need for corroborative evidence put some defendants into a strong position. Between 1870 and 1914, failure to meet the evidence standard accounted for 21 per cent of unsuccessful claims and women without written proof of an offer of marriage usually failed to establish their case in law. Viewed objectively, the balance of probability in several of these cases lay with the woman. Although some men were clearly victims of spurious claims before 1869 because of the low standards of evidence accepted by the courts, far more women appear to have suffered after 1870 because of the exceptionally high standard they had to meet.

Whilst the evidence requirements were being slowly worked out by judges, the fraud that they were intended to guard against continued unabated, and, according to contemporaries, intensified. Until the mid-1860s, false claims appear to have been brought by casual opportunists, who usually connived with family or friends on a one-off basis to relieve a rich man of some money. Harriet Spicer, who lost her case in 1865, may have been the first professional fraudster to pursue a man in the courtroom. Direct evidence of extortion is necessarily shadowy, but critics of breach of promise regularly cited the same handful of cases to illustrate their contention that men were being blackmailed with threats of court action, perhaps suggesting that the crime was not as pervasive as was being alleged.

However, it is noticeable that more unsuccessful claims were reported in 1870s newspapers than in other decades. At least one of these plaintiffs had previously settled another breach of promise claim by agreement. To lose one bridegroom might be considered a misfortune, but to lose two, or even three, seems like more than carelessness. At least two verdicts were quashed when the defendant proved that the woman had lied to achieve her victory. Until the Appeal Court established what was acceptable corroboration of a promise to wed, the evidence reforms gave a dishonest woman the opportunity to fabricate and present a spurious claim in court, instead of having to persuade a witness to speak for her.

One case overlooked by contemporaries was that brought by 22-year-old Alice Chick. In November 1878 her claim would have sounded depressingly familiar to those in court. Four years earlier she had met a respectable gentleman on a London street and they began a friendship. After several weeks he offered marriage to entice her into sexual intimacy, and then abandoned her the following morning. Nine months later Alice became a mother. The judge remarked that the case lacked any corroboration of a promise to marry, but as the defendant had not acknowledged the claim or provided any defence he allowed this silence to confirm Alice's story.

A few weeks later, on Christmas Day, Michael MacCauliffe, a Deputy Commissioner in the Punjab, picked up his morning newspaper and read that Alice Chick had been awarded £400 for his breach of promise. This was the first he knew of the case and was a complete shock to him as he knew no-one named Alice Chick. He had been sailing to India when her solicitors began the claim and had never received any papers from the court. Perplexed, and disgraced in the eyes of those who knew him, MacCauliffe returned to England to try and discover why Alice thought he was the man who had seduced her. He persuaded a reluctant judge to set aside the verdict and grant him a new hearing, though only on condition that he paid £400 into court to protect Alice's interests. The judge felt it unlikely that another jury would believe his defence.

There was no second trial. In August 1879, *The Times* printed a letter from MacCauliffe stating that Alice had given him written exoneration from the conduct she had accused him of in court and that, as a consequence, he had dropped a prosecution for criminal perjury against her.

The case was one of mistaken identity and it seems probable that Alice's solicitor knowingly assisted her to bring a false claim. When Alice first took legal advice she named the man who abandoned her as an army captain called George MacCauley. The solicitor traced MacCauliffe, probably through a private investigator, and Alice identified her missing seducer from a photograph. It is possible that Alice could have made a genuine mistake. Perhaps more likely is that her solicitor thought that a senior civil servant earning £1,300 was a better prospect for damages than an officer earning around £300 a year and convinced her to claim against the wrong man.

By 1879, there were considerable misgivings among the middle-classes about breach of promise claims. Influential opinion had polarised with some sections of the establishment calling for the claim to be ended, whilst others fervently supported it. In 1872, when John Hawkins's barrister expressed the hope that some day breach of promise actions would be abolished, Mr Justice Quain retorted that if that day ever came, he hoped any man who treated a woman in a shameful way and broke his promise without cause would feel the weight of the criminal law instead.

In May 1879, supporters and opponents locked horns when Farrer Herschell, a leading barrister, and the Liberal MP for the City of Durham, proposed a motion in the House of Commons to restrict damages in breach of promise claims to the actual losses suffered as a result of relying on the promise, such as the wasted cost of wedding preparations. Introducing the debate, Herschell identified that breach of promise 'stuck its roots deeper into the social system and trawled the life of society at more points than would at first sight appear', and illustrated this with a wide-ranging critique of the negative aspects of breach of promise, as perceived by upper-middle class, male society.

Herschell argued that modest and decent women, however badly-treated by a man, would not sully themselves by baring their feelings in a public court for financial compensation. He thought that women who brought claims were using it as a way to extort money, pointing out that it was impossible to place a financial value on hurt feelings and the loss of marriage. Drawing on his practical experiences as an advocate, Herschell was well-placed to explain how the courts treated a man who decided to defend a claim. He pointed out that the merest hint that a woman was anything but a collection of all the female virtues, or had given her fiancé any reason to reconsider his promise, brought down a torrent of invective from the plaintiff's counsel and the judge and risked the displeasure of the jury in a heavy award of damages.

Herschell also exposed the unpleasant side of Victorian attitudes towards beauty and money. He explained how a pretty woman with a good chance of another engagement received far higher damages than a plain woman whose loss was probably greater, as her chances of attracting another suitor were much lower. This was a reversal of the apparent fairness demonstrated by a Leicestershire jury in 1817, who pointedly answered the question 'will you give as great a price for a homely piece of goods as for the finest commodity?' by awarding plain Mary Cooper £1,000.

Equally unpalatable to the modern mind, though certainly

in keeping with the views of Charles Dickens, was Hershell's revelation that legal professionals had voiced self-interested opposition to restricting the scope of breach of promise because they objected 'to the loss of such cases in a season of such depression of trade'. As Herschell pointed out, providing a living for legal professionals was not a justification for retaining any law.

Members of the House of Commons backed Herschell's call for reform of a law that was 'scandalously abused' by 106 votes to 65. A few months later, barrister Charles McColla published a short and influential book about the history and social considerations relating to breach of promise. McColla reiterated the points made by Herschell and added much more detail about frauds and misuse of the claim, even suggesting that the lovers' leap could be as effective as money in curing broken hearts. Herschell and McColla were accurate in their analyses of the many problems attached to breach of promise claims, but the points they made were not criticisms of a bad law but of a law that was operated badly.

Despite contemporary belief, middle-class ladies did recover damages for broken engagements, usually through a private settlement rather than by parading their feelings in court. The law could deal with fraud and extortion with a period of unpleasant imprisonment. Men who gave in to blackmail may have considered themselves stuck between a rock and a hard place, but giving in was their choice. *The Observer* acknowledged that 'there are certain circumstances under which a man who has regard for his own reputation will rather pay blackmail than allow the story of his own folly to be made public'. It was usually choice rather than chance that led a prosperous man to become entangled with a lower-class woman, with several defendants having initiated the relationship by striking up a conversation with a woman in the street.

Women who enforced their legal right to compensation after a broken engagement, however distasteful to the defendant or wider society, were not committing any crime, a point critics sometimes seem to have overlooked when branding them extortioners. In some cases the woman was out-of-pocket because of the defendant's broken promise and the damages were not necessarily great once she had been reimbursed for this. Other problems arose from the legal system itself. Placing a financial value on a lost marriage was difficult, but judges could have addressed the scandal of unrealistic awards of damages, rather than turning away when defendants asked for clearly excessive sums to be reduced. Penalising a man for criticising a woman when defending her claim, condoning impudent claims and awarding damages based on beauty were failings of jurors rather than of any law.

Although Herschell won his debate this did not lead to a change in the law. On four separate occasions between 1881 and 1890 individual MPs each sponsored a Private Member's Bill, but such bills rarely succeed unless there is substantial consensus about the desirability of change and tacit support or direct help from the government. Many establishment figures were strong supporters of a woman's right to bring a claim for breach of promise. They believed the claim protected women from exploitation by discouraging men from uttering pledges they had no intention of keeping or of changing their mind capriciously.

The availability of damages made men think carefully about their actions and might indirectly prevent women from having to claim public assistance. A woman who withdrew from the marriage market could lose out on other opportunities to find a husband and provider. One who gave up her job only to be jilted might struggle to find other employment. Women who wasted money on abortive wedding preparations could have saved their limited resources for a rainy day. Those who had given birth to an illegitimate child after being seduced under a promise of marriage, used the claim to obtain a lump sum to help with child maintenance.

How much of the establishment's attitude related to protecting economically disadvantaged working-class women and how much of it related to controlling any perceived promiscuous impulses of less affluent males is unclear. It seems likely that social control, rather than any respect for the female gender, was the reason establishment figures opposed the half-hearted attempts at reform in the 1880s. The Appeal Court showed little regard for working-class women who brought claims against wealthy men.

In the 1880s, breach of promise began a further period of change, possibly linked to Herschell's and McColla's pointed criticisms. Barristers gradually toned down the rhetoric about a woman's disappointed hopes or a man's heartless conduct. Judges regularly advised juries to ensure that damages were not out of proportion to the parties' status in life and to take account of what the man could afford to pay.

As damages became a little more aligned with a defendant's means, it became apparent that a few women were motivated by vengeance alone; a point an occasional plaintiff acknowledged from the witness box. In 1896, Ellen Jones received just £25 from printer's manager, James Wilson, in a claim of barely-concealed revenge. Ellen acknowledged that they were an incompatible pair, describing their many quarrels as 'six of one and half a dozen of the other'. Wilson said that when he asked her to consider whether they really could be happy together, Ellen had threatened to make trouble for him and his parents if he broke the engagement. By the time the claim was heard she had already been courted by someone else.

Given the few opportunities working-class women had to support themselves in any degree of comfort it is unsurprising that those who had a claim for breach of promise tried to improve their financial security. Some had no option but to take a man to court if he had cost them money or refused to negotiate a fair settlement. Nor is it always easy to condemn an impoverished woman for succumbing to the temptation to make a few pounds from blackmail or extortion if the opportunity presented itself or a rich man wanted to keep his bad conduct a secret. Middle-class observers frequently criticised working-class women as unladylike and grasping for exposing their feelings in public in order to obtain damages, but failed to notice that women from their own class were also motivated by greed and opportunism.

Gertrude Ricketts, the daughter of an army officer, obtained substantial damages from two men. In 1892, she settled a claim privately, receiving £1,000 from a now unknown man. Whilst visiting India in 1901 she embarked on a second romance, clearly determined that if she did not land her army captain, then she would land the money she thought he had. Gertrude was described as 'a spider weaving a web for an unwary fly' for the businesslike approach she adopted throughout her courtship by Thomas Gaskell, making copies of all her letters before she posted them and carefully dating any she received from him.

In 1903, a London jury awarded her £1,500, which forced Gaskell to apply for bankruptcy a few weeks later. His total assets were less than £62. When he applied for his discharge from bankruptcy later that year Gertrude opposed it, because she had not received her money. Gertrude said that she would accept payment by instalments from his army pay, a solution Gaskell rejected because most of his salary was swallowed up by regimental charges for accommodation and food. The judge postponed any decision about Gaskell at this point, indicating that he ought to pay at least £600.

The unresolved situation then disappeared from the news and no further information about Gaskell has been located, raising the possibility that he either changed his name or left the country to escape damages he could not afford. Despite the disappointment of mistaking Gaskell's actual wealth, Gertrude was not left in a difficult financial situation because of her broken engagement. As an officer's daughter, she enjoyed a pension of £60 a year, which makes the dogged manner in which she pursued Gaskell for money he did not have particularly unpleasant.

Gertrude was one of a declining number of women bringing a claim for breach of promise when she took court action. Although public distaste had not reduced claims, by the twentieth century awards of low damages may have had this effect. Added to this, intellectual women were critical of the action, considering that the special favour it bestowed on females was contrary to gender equality and promoted marriage as a woman's career.

During the Edwardian age, the combination of low awards and better educational and employment opportunities for women contributed to breach of promise becoming a very tawdry action. For 18 cases mentioned in newspapers in 1914, the lack of detail highlights the contempt many felt for those who brought claims. One was fraudulently brought by a married woman, who was jailed for aggravated perjury a few months later, whilst another couple had cohabited for 26 years until he married someone else. The highest damages were £500, awarded to two women whose claims had aggravating elements. Two women received a similar sum though negotiation. A bad-tempered woman received only a farthing, the smallest coin of the realm, as her tantrums had prompted her fiancé to have second thoughts.

Breach of promise claims continued throughout the Great War, although at a very low rate; a surprising reminder that life went on away from the scenes of carnage and some men never saw active service. Spring 1915 produced a very unusual case, which demonstrates how little those who were not involved in combat understood its realities at that point. A defendant, Lieutenant James Montague Coutts Duffus, had been mobilised for active service, obliging the War Office to send a telegram to court stating that Duffus could not attend the hearing as he could not be spared from his battery. On receipt of the telegram, the presiding judge adjourned the case until the end of the war. There is no indication that the case was brought before a jury when Duffus returned from the trenches.

The number of breach of promise claims began to increase in 1919, but this did not presage a return to the pre-war situation: the public mood had changed. Women suing for money they had spent on wedding preparations sometimes failed to recover all of it. Two women won cases, but only gained a farthing in damages and were told by scathing judges that their claims were against public policy or offended the feelings of right-thinking people. The only women who appear to have recovered good levels of damages were in cases with aggravating conduct by the defendant. In 1921, Mr Justice McCardie stated in court that breach of promise law should be reviewed, as two-thirds of claims were not brought to rectify a loss but to inflict public hurt on a man who had disappointed a woman. He awarded Minnie Sutton just £25 for the expenses she had incurred while preparing for marriage and for Sydney Pearce's unmanly conduct, but refused to compensate her for matrimonial loss, stating that a hot-tempered woman and a man addicted to alcohol would have enjoyed no happiness in any case.

By 1923, a combination of public scorn, contemptuous damages and being denied their legal costs had forced most vengeful or vexatious claimants out of the courtroom. In cases where a plaintiff was suing to recover money she had spent, damages tended to be restricted to the actual financial losses caused by the defendant's breach, with no awards for hurt feelings or future expectations, unless the defendant had behaved in a disgraceful way. Woman who were seduced under a promise of marriage, whether or not they became pregnant, continued to receive substantial awards, as did Doris Hartley, whose wealthy fiancé ended their engagement when her father lost money.

Several cases were brought to resolve specific issues which had arisen from a broken engagement and some were decided in the highest courts in the land. These included splitting the assets of a bigamous marriage, ensuring provision for illegitimate children who were not being maintained and resolving property disputes, such as the ownership of the engagement ring. The one that most interested the press was the claim by Emily Fender, a young nurse who had accepted a proposal from a divorcing man. She became formally engaged to Sir Anthony Mildmay after the decree nisi was issued, but before his divorce was made absolute. Judges decided that when a decree nisi had been issued a marriage was effectively dissolved and a plaintiff could rely on a promise made at this point, allowing Emily to receive damages of £2,000 in 1937.

Public disquiet again emerged in the mid-1930s, with occasional parliamentary questions and reform proposals in the press, linked to a belief that breach of promise was increasingly being used as an instrument of extortion. In 1935, Harold Blakeley, a retired cotton merchant, paid Margaret Hope £400 because he did not want his name in the papers. After investing the money she tried to obtain more, alleging that he had proposed to her a second time. Blakeley accepted the inevitable publicity and defended her claim. The jury found in his favour. Damages too were becoming a cause of concern, with *The Guardian* drawing attention to an award of £158 against a man who earned less than £3 a week. This was more than his annual income.

One of the first government actions when Britain went to war in 1939 was to suspend jury trials in civil cases. A trickle of breach of promise claims were heard by a judge who decided the damages. Reports show that these hearings had a no-nonsense quality; judges were not about to agonise over hurting a woman's feelings with harsh comments about her motives or sending a man into bankruptcy because he had exaggerated his means. When jury trials resumed in the late 1940s, claims were usually brought by foreign women, older women and women who had been lured into sexual relationships believing in a promise of marriage.

Older women tended to be survivors of bigamous marriages. As these were invalid, property and inheritance law could offer no help when a woman discovered after her man's death that she was not, in law, his widow and had no right to support from his estate. Breach of promise law adapted and helped them. Sensible and sympathetic reasoning by judges in the Appeal Court established that anyone who entered a bigamous marriage could obtain damages, the amount being the jury's pragmatic assessment of what was appropriate in the circumstances. In some cases this was a few thousand pounds.

By 1960, MPs were again questioning the relevance of breach of promise in a modern society, though with no public clamour for change, the Conservative government did not consider it a priority for reform. The impetus for review came in 1965 after the new Labour government set up the Law Commission, whose functions included ascertaining whether laws were up-to-date. The Commission decided to review breach of promise because it seemed to rest on out-dated social assumptions.

In October 1969, Commissioners recommended abolishing breach of promise. Public consultation had confirmed that many people thought it was a charter for gold-diggers, or a legal substitute for a shotgun in its power to coerce a reluctant groom to the altar. These criticisms were perceptions of problems rather than reflecting wide-spread practice, but the Commission concluded that the stability of marriage was important to society and it was inappropriate for public policy to sanction the threat of legal action to push unwilling people into a marriage. The Commission recognised that abolishing the claim would be unfair in the situations where it solved practical problems arising from some failed engagements and recommended that any reform should include provision for dealing with property issues and for maintaining the survivors of a bigamous marriage. It also recommended the abolition of other obsolete claims which treated a person as someone else's property.

During 1970, the Legal Reform (Miscellaneous Provisions) Bill was considered in Parliament and passed into law as:

An Act to abolish actions for breach of promise of marriage and make provision with respect to the property of, and gifts between, persons who have been engaged to marry; to abolish the right of a husband to claim damages for adultery with his wife; to abolish actions for the enticement or harbouring of a spouse, or for the enticement, seduction or harbouring of a child; to make provision with respect to the maintenance of survivors of void marriages; and for purposes connected with the matters aforesaid.

From 1 January 1971 it was impossible for either party to recover wasted expenditure on wedding arrangements or for a woman to be compensated for seduction or pregnancy. Child maintenance law no longer restricted what the father of an illegitimate child could be required to pay, so breach of promise damages were not needed to supplement the father's contribution. Spouses who had unknowingly entered a bigamous marriage could bring claims for maintenance, and property disputes between engaged couples were to be dealt with as though they had been married. An engagement ring was confirmed as an unconditional gift to the woman, unless a man had stipulated any conditions when he gave it. The only breach of promise cases that remained to be heard were those where court action had already been started. The last was heard in May 1971.

Eighty-six words swept away more than three centuries of history. They brought to an end a claim which, in 1803, had been described as one of 'great discrimination and diversity'. Although breach of promise had been denigrated and despised since the 1830s, it had etched a very unusual place in the fabric of English society. Some of its earliest beneficiaries were middle-class ladies, but in the class-conscious nineteenth century, it increasingly provided an effective redress for working-class women at a time when poor women struggled under the double disadvantage of gender and class. It was a very flexible claim, adaptable to changing social circumstances, and able to offer protection to those who fell outside the scope of other laws. Its much mooted demise only occurred when women no longer needed it.

By 1971, gender assumptions were breaking down and children's rights to maintenance had been improved. A country that had once viewed marriage as a commercial contract now saw it as a state to be entered into willingly by both parties and attached no public disgrace to a jilted woman, if a man decided, for any reason, that he could not honour a commitment to make her his wife.

Chapter 4

ALL THE WORLD'S A STAGE
THE LEGAL SYSTEM AND BREACH OF PROMISE

"They said what a wery gen'rous thing it was o' them to have taken the case 'on spec', and to charge nothin' at all for costs, unless they got 'em out of Mr Pickwick".
(Charles Dickens, *The Pickwick Papers*, 1837)

Although nineteenth century men saw themselves as the stronger sex, when it came to a breach of promise claim, gender assumptions were often reversed. Most men preferred to avoid the court room and those who wished to extricate themselves from an engagement were usually prepared to agree a private arrangement. This was cheaper, more discreet and would not expose a man as a dishonourable cad who had forced his former fiancée to bring a public claim for recompense. It is probable that there was always a dubious aspect to any claims heard in court, which would account for the distasteful connotations surrounding breach of promise from an early stage.

Information about settlements negotiated out-of-court is scarce because they were not in the public domain, but what does exist suggests that women could obtain handsome payments. It is likely that some well-bred ladies had their damages decided in court solely because they, or their families, had made unrealistic demands for compensation, rather than because a wealthy man had refused to do the decent thing. In 1825, defendant George Horton publicly criticised the family of 19-year-old Margaret Capper for dragging her name into court, rather than settling. The damages of £1,000 that the jury awarded to Margaret may have been lower than the offer her family had rejected, as Horton's fortune was around £24,000.

Breach of promise claims were brought, nominally, by the

person who had been jilted. If the plaintiff was under 21, a parent or guardian had to bring the claim on their behalf and the young woman probably enjoyed little, if any, influence over decisions taken in her name. Plaintiffs who were old enough to sue in court may have been firmly steered by senior relatives and allowed no unfettered choice over the course taken.

Before a claim arrived in court it had passed through several informal stages. The first of these was taking legal advice, and by 1820 there was no shortage of eager solicitors (known as attorneys at this time), to smooth a woman's path into the courtroom. Small towns had at least one solicitor and he was usually willing to offer a brief consultation and scrutinise letters for evidence of a promise of marriage. Respectable solicitors made their living from identifying laws that had been broken and then facilitating a claim for damages. Others were more pro-active in attracting business, and provided women with safe storage facilities for compromising letters until news arrived that a deserting fiancé had married someone else. A few used pushy and aggressive tactics, and one London firm of solicitors appears to have employed private detectives to locate missing fiancés.

Access to the courts was not free and a woman could only bring a claim if she could pay her legal bills. These varied according to the circumstances of the breach, how much time was spent trying to resolve the claim privately and the fees charged by her advisors. Legal costs are shrouded in secrecy as very few cases provide details about the fees incurred. Middle-class ladies with money at their disposal engaged solicitors with a sound reputation, and sometimes retained a barrister to help with any negotiations. Their legal bills could amount to hundreds of pounds. Poor women with no savings were obliged to find a cheap solicitor, and try to persuade a friend or relative to loan money or stand as a guarantor for the legal costs.

The high success rate of women in breach of promise cases led to some solicitors covertly offering what are now termed no-win-no-fee deals, known at the time as taking a case 'on spec'. Direct evidence of the practice dates from 1850, when a solicitor named Webber sued John Symes and his new wife, Matilda, for the balance of the costs she had incurred in a breach of promise case against another man two years earlier. She won, but received just a farthing in damages and was refused her legal costs, leaving Webber £81 out-of-pocket on his gamble. He remained out-of-pocket, as the judge ruled that he had offered his services on a 'no-cure-no-pay' basis and had no claim against his former client.

Conditional fees were on the margins of legality in the nineteenth century and were offered at the lawyer's discretion when a woman with a strong case could not afford to take it to court, depriving the lawyer of the money he could earn for helping with her claim. As the person who lost a court case was usually ordered to pay the legal costs incurred by the winner, the solicitor advising a successful woman would obtain his payment from the defendant, not from his client.

Several cases brought by poor women indicate that the solicitor collected an up-front deposit of around £20 from the plaintiff before beginning any work on the claim. This would cover the costs of correspondence with the defendant and court fees, and probably placed the solicitor's services on the correct side of legality. A very small number of solicitors may have strayed into an illegal arrangement known as champerty; claiming a fee and a proportion of the damages recovered.

Not all women were offered a no-win-no-fee arrangement. Fee-chasing solicitors were not interested in justice but in claims that did not expose them to risk; taking up cases where they could guarantee victory for the plaintiff, by proving that a promise had been made and broken. This explains why more than a third of all claims for breach of promise were not made until the defendant had married someone else or had written to the woman to break the engagement, as this made the broken promise impossible to deny, leaving the amount of damages the only question for the jury to decide.

To obtain a fee, unprincipled solicitors encouraged women to bring very dubious claims, holding out the unrealistic prospect of winning £100 or more, even when it must have been obvious that the woman would receive derisory damages and be exposed to public ridicule in the process. Several cases disparaged in court as 'attorney's actions' garnered only a few pounds in compensation, as juries chivalrously awarded the woman just enough money to ensure that she would not be ordered to pay the defendant's legal costs or be harassed to pay her own.

Although some no-win-no-fee cases show a sordid side to breach of promise claims, they also provided poor women with access to the law. Knowing that some solicitors would take a claim 'on spec' may have made men think twice about a proposal they had no intention of honouring and probably induced men who had changed their minds to offer realistic out-of-court settlements. Convincing a solicitor of the strength of her case was perhaps the hardest hurdle a poor woman had to clear, as a solicitor would only begin work on a case when he was satisfied that either the plaintiff or the defendant would be paying his bills.

The opening gambit in a breach of promise claim was a letter to the defendant, pointing out that he had failed to meet his obligations to his fiancée and enquiring what compensation he was prepared to pay her to avoid the unpleasantness of a claim for breach of promise. At this point the defendant usually hurried to a solicitor of his own, but some, whether out of inertia or because they considered the claim was an idle threat, ignored all communication until court action was imminent. If the defendant retained a solicitor, then letters flew between both lawyers, ranging from an instantaneous rebuttal of the claim to an offer to negotiate mutually acceptable compensation.

There are no records of how many claims were compromised and how many were abandoned at this stage, but any claim that could be defended would be rooted out aggressively by the plaintiff's solicitor if he had offered a 'no-cure-no-pay' deal. A solicitor would decide whether to help a woman with a weak claim negotiate a settlement, or wash his hands of her, based on what he could obtain for himself. This probably accounts for the very high success rate of breach of promise plaintiffs as it prevented weak or frivolous cases reaching court. Women who could not afford legal fees had no autonomy over how their claims were treated.

If a valid claim existed, settling it informally was an exercise in brinkmanship for both sides. Defendants had to consider the cost of two sets of legal fees in addition to damages when deciding whether to settle. Plaintiffs had to weigh up whether to accept a lower offer than they were dreaming of or to gamble that the jury would be generous. Unless the proof of a promise was incontrovertible and the woman had sustained real harm from it being broken, there was always the chance that a jury would be unsympathetic. Occasionally, the amount the plaintiff had refused was mentioned in court. Most juries matched or bettered this offer, but some did not. In 1874, Susan Tredwell refused an annuity of £50 and obtained £300, rather than the £1,300 she stated as her loss. Minnie Sewell, who turned down £500 in 1900, was awarded only £300 by the jury.

If no settlement could be reached informally, the plaintiff's solicitor drew up the paperwork and began court proceedings. The Royal Courts of Justice were based in London and all legal cases were started in one of its four divisions. There were no rules about which division dealt with a breach of promise claim and solicitors used their personal preference. Most claims began in either the Court of the King's (or Queen's) Bench, or the Court of Common Pleas, but a few were taken to the Court of Exchequer which dealt with financial matters. As part of a series of wide-ranging reforms, the divisions of Common Pleas and Exchequer were abolished in 1880 and all breach of promise claims were considered by the Court of the Queen's Bench. Scotland had its own legal system which dealt with claims stated there.

Geography determined where a claim was heard. Those relating to London were usually heard in the Courts of Justice, while cases which originated in other areas were heard by the next Assize Court. Plaintiffs could determine where their case was heard and some ensured that their case was heard in London; a practice that might raise questions about why they were avoiding a local hearing. Sinister motives were often imputed to plaintiffs, but some may have simply preferred not to wash dirty linen in front of leering acquaintances. A surprising number of couples had met whilst both were away from home, working or visiting relatives, making it difficult to know which was the most appropriate venue.

Assize courts were usually held in spring and summer by judges from the London courts who toured the main provincial towns, spending a few days in each hearing serious criminal cases and civil claims. The Assizes were a popular highlight of early nineteenth century provincial life across all social classes. Lists of the cases to be heard were published in advance, and local people treated Assize days as an unofficial holiday, flocking in from surrounding districts to be entertained by interesting or scandalous cases. When Mary Orford's claim was heard in 1818, the press reported a crowd of 2,000 people in Lancaster Castle. The most vibrant descriptions of breach of promise cases are from provincial Assizes. In London, where courts sat regularly and other forms of public entertainment were readily available, crowds only packed a courtroom to bursting point when particularly embarrassing revelations or large damages were anticipated.

Even though the Assizes had the outward appearance of a public holiday, solicitors had no time to relax. When a case was listed for hearing, solicitors for the plaintiff and the defendant had to arrange for a barrister to present the case in court. Barristers were self-employed, highly trained legal advocates whose role was to represent a client's interest by highlighting the strengths of their case and trying to undermine any arguments put forward by the other party.

Wealthy plaintiffs and defendants usually commissioned an early opinion on their case from a barrister with expertise in breach of promise. He would study all the information collated by the solicitor and might become involved in negotiating an informal settlement. Poorer people had to be content with a quick reading of their paperwork by any barrister who happened to be in town, irrespective of his competence or experience. Barristers who followed the Assizes as they toured the country were often in the early stages of their careers and trying to build up a reputation. For a barrister, breach of promise claims were usually straightforward to present or defend with little prior knowledge, as they followed a standard form, using a standard patter.

Occasionally, barristers who presented cases they knew little about, found themselves in embarrassing situations, as solicitors could conceal inconvenient facts to secure representation for their client. More than one barrister resigned from the case in court to protect his own reputation when he discovered that he had been deceived about the plaintiff he was representing or that her claim was fraudulent.

Very occasionally, a plaintiff or defendant represented themselves in court. Men were motivated by saving legal costs when they acknowledged a broken engagement. The women who presented their own cases usually had weak claims and probably could not afford to pay an advocate or secure one 'on spec'.

As soon as a barrister became involved, a further opportunity to settle arose and around two per cent of cases listed for hearing were resolved before the case was called into court. This probably reflects objective assessment by both barristers of how much a jury was likely to award. Interestingly, settlements with no compromise were obtained at this late stage by both parties, suggesting that one of the attorneys had given poor advice to their client. In 1893, Miss Samwans received £2,000, the full amount she had initially asked for, while in 1896, Miss Algar's claim against Mr Lewis was settled for no damages and without costs, indicating that both barristers regarded it as fraudulent.

When a case was ushered into the courtroom, detailed information about it entered the public domain and was recorded verbatim by legal clerks and journalists using shorthand. This skill formed part of a university education, but it could also be self-taught by a determined individual, such as Charles Dickens, keen to increase his earning capacity. Until the mid-nineteenth century, the most sensational cases were published word for word in pamphlet form and sold, either to a voracious public, or to solicitors eager to know what decisions were being taken in courts across the country. Many more cases were reported in abridged form by newspapers, providing a wealth of detail about the claims, and revealing the social attitudes of the era.

From a historian's perspective, the clerk or journalist who sat quietly recording the proceedings was the most important person in court, as without their diligent scribing, few traces of the claim for breach of promise of marriage would remain. Extant legal records cover comparatively few of the claims heard in court and often they note the new or the unusual rather than the commonplace, and capture the legal thinking of senior judges rather than the actions of participants.

Early newspapers did not credit contributors with by-lines, so court reporters are largely anonymous unless, like Dickens, they became illustrious for some reason. There were two types of reporter; salaried employees and freelance contributors.

Identical reports in the early decades of the nineteenth century can be found in unrelated newspapers, suggesting authorship by an enterprising freelance writer. On other occasions, even allowing for editing, reports of a case differ sufficiently in detail and emphasis to indicate that they did not originate from the same source. Freelance contributors may have been more usual at the provincial Assizes, possibly providing material to a regional paper and sending reports of the more interesting cases to the nationals. This would have been a more practical method for national newspapers to obtain copy than sending salaried staff to the provinces, on the off-chance that a newsworthy case would be heard. Some early reports were provided to the press by enterprising law firms, from the notes written by their clerks.

***

In the early decades of the nineteenth century, breach of promise trials ranked alongside cases of seduction and criminal conversation and regularly attracted large, raucous crowds. For many years newspapers commented on jostling crowds and the inability of the police or court officials to control pushing and shoving. Health and safety had not yet become a consideration, though no reports of injury were noted either. The promise of embarrassing revelations about the amorous misadventures of a man who was wealthy, old, supposedly respectable or had fathered the woman's child proved a magnet to all social classes and women as well as men jostled to take their place in the audience. In March 1826, when the Stafford Assizes heard a claim by Etty Peake, against John Wedgwood, a member of the famous pottery dynasty, *The Observer* reported:

> *As early as seven o'clock in the morning, groups of well-dressed persons of both sexes were collected round the Town Hall, and on the opening of the Court, every place and avenue were crammed full. The heat was so intense in Court that the breath of the crowd condensed on the stone roof of the hall was continually showering down upon those below.*

Public interest in Etty's case arose because of the standing of the defendant and the expectation that she would receive high damages. In the event, the young widow was awarded £1,500 to popular approval. Society was sharply divided by class and wealth and many people saw a woman's triumph against a privileged man as a victory for the underdog. Audiences often cheered when high damages were awarded.

When a case was known to involve sexual scandal, large audiences were guaranteed and women displayed no prudery when a case was of an indelicate nature, though some judges adopted a protective stance towards them. In 1820, Mr Justice Parke ordered the women and boys of Carlisle to withdraw from court because Jane Lawson's claim involved seduction and the birth of an illegitimate child. Six years later, the more liberal Mr Justice Garrow told the throng of ladies in the courtroom when a seduction case was called that he did not desire them to wait in court to hear anything that may shock their modesty; unless they chose to remain. A couple of ladies retired at that point, but the great majority stayed, eager to hear the case. By 1890, notions of respectable public conduct for a lady had changed. Miss Harris's claim also involved seduction and an illegitimate child, and when the judge warned that the case would contain sordid details all the women in court took his advice to leave.

It could take some time for the crowd to settle, and courts sometimes opened their doors early to allow for this, but once everyone was assembled, the hearing began. Straightforward cases and those undefended were concluded in a few hours. Those where the defendant refuted the plaintiff's claims might need a full day to get through the evidence and particularly complex ones could run to three or four days. In presenting the case, both barristers treated the courtroom as a theatre and shamelessly played to the gallery, and more specifically to the twelve jurors. The case opened with a prologue as the plaintiff's barrister outlined her claim. Although it would have sounded original and convincing to inexperienced lay jurors, this usually florid and impassioned opening speech rarely deviated from a standard script about a paragon of virtue who had been wronged by a grievous injury the like of which words could not describe.

If opening speeches are taken at face value, all middle-class women who suffered disappointment in love were beautiful, accomplished and ladylike and all poor ones were modest and from respectable families. Amelia Wharton 'had been carefully brought up in the strictest morals and she possessed great personal attractions'. Sarah Rose was 'a young lady of considerable beauty and accomplishments', whilst Margaret Capper was 'a young lady of great beauty and accomplishments', and Keziah Langley excelled as 'a young lady of good education, great beauty, some accomplishments and not without respectability of birth'.

In the early nineteenth century, it was unusual for a plaintiff to attend court in person as she could take no part in the proceedings. In 1801, Miss Vaughan's case may have suffered when she was spotted in the public gallery, impatient to hear how much of the defendant's money she would obtain. If a woman wished to be in court it was better if she sat openly with her legal team. In 1819, newspapers noted Maria Spenser sitting behind her lawyers. A few weeks later, a journalist's description of Esther Dawson's beauty was not a barrister's insincere effusion, strongly suggesting that she had adopted a similar seat. Their barristers may have requested this, so that they could quickly refute anticipated denials or character attacks by the defendant's witnesses. In many cases it would have been advantageous for a plaintiff not to be present. Rhetoric about beauty, charm, refinement and grief could be undermined if the defendant's barrister spotted a plain woman who was laughing.

The practice of women sitting in court was more usual by the 1830s and canny lawyers took advantage of this by advising their client to present a modest and ladylike demeanour and how to gain the sympathy of the jury. In the 1870s, when women were first allowed to give evidence, some appeared in their wedding outfit, demonstrating that they envisaged no further use for it, or in deep mourning to symbolise their loss. Ellen Kelly was 'a prepossessing young woman attired in deep mourning' and Amelia Potts 'a middle-aged lady dressed in black satin'. It is unclear when the fad ceased, as newspaper reports of breach of promise cases after the mid-1890s became brief and factual to the point of contempt.

Once the woman's barrister had established her many virtues and broken heart in the minds of the jurors, the drama began in earnest. Act One belonged to the plaintiff as her barrister called witnesses and produced evidence to confirm the story he had already told; to prove that the woman had expected the defendant to marry her; and that he had refused to honour his word. This was the part of the hearing that the audience relished, because it often involved the reading of letters written by the defendant, and sometimes a barrister made an ironic apology for disappointing the crowd when there were no letters to be read. As poems and pet names and expressions of undying love poured from the barrister's lips, hearings were punctuated with bursts of laughter from those crowded into court. Adding to the defendant's often considerable embarrassment, newspapers reported these in detail. Almost two hundred years later, perusing some of these letters in newspaper reports feels uncomfortable and voyeuristic.

The practice of reading letters in court was always questionable, except when this was the only way of proving that the defendant had offered marriage. The alleged justification for reading from private correspondence was to show the close relationship that had once existed between the plaintiff and defendant. In reality, letters were a powerful negotiating tool and some defendants were prepared to settle a case in order to prevent their indiscreet words being read out and then published in the press. In 1828, a judge asked newspapers not to print any details from the letters of a 76-year-old linen draper to a 64-year-old widow who had entrapped him. In an age when the press was liable to face a range of curbs on its existence if it defied figures of authority, the editors respected his request.

Over time, judges became increasingly circumspect about what private correspondence could be read aloud and generally refused to hear anything that did not contain a reference to marriage. Despite this, the distasteful tactic of trying to embarrass or punish a man by reading from his letters continued well into the twentieth century, though by that time the press had stopped reporting the details.

In addition to letters, most plaintiffs had at least one witness who could confirm their engagement and the circumstances of it being broken. Witnesses were sometimes asked about the defendant's finances and standard of living to assist the jury in deciding what the plaintiff had lost. Any witness evidence could be tested by the defendant's barrister who often focussed upon the plaintiff's reaction to the broken engagement, trying to establish how upset she really was.

Plaintiffs who gave evidence were treated solicitously. In 1881, middle-class Kate Lamb was allowed to sit while she told her story. Women rarely faced harsh cross-examination as causing a woman any distress might provoke a jury to award her exemplary damages. For less educated women, speaking from the witness box could be a disservice, as any solecism or deviation from middle-class moral standards could perhaps contribute to the impression that she did not deserve substantial compensation. Ann Letts, a 54-year-old widow, caused laughter in a Liverpool courtroom after replying 207, when asked her age, thinking that she had been told to give her house number. She obtained a farthing in 1873 from John McGrath; particularly contemptuous treatment by the jury given that McGrath had used a promise of marriage he had no intention of honouring to borrow money from her and was proving evasive about paying it back.

In 1878, Ann Sutton lost her claim against Thomas Lucas after some of her letters were read out in court. Questioned about the disgusting content, she replied that her letters were no worse than his. At this point, the judge intervened, saying that 'it was not desirable that a contest of indecency should take place in the court room', and stopped the hearing, ruling that Ann could not recover any damages even if she established a broken engagement.

When the plaintiff's witnesses had been heard, Act Two was directed by the defendant's barrister, who pleaded his client's case. Men who attended court also followed conventions about their appearance, attempting to look as poor and foolish as possible to keep damages to a minimum. Defendants regularly turned up ungroomed, probably unwashed, and wearing their shabbiest clothing. In 1870, an unwary Robert Ensor found himself admitting to Annie Jones's barrister that he had a better jacket and trousers at home. Barristers quickly discovered that it was unwise for a defendant to give evidence and rarely took the risk of allowing the defendant to speak as he then faced cross-examination by the plaintiff's legal team. No holds were barred in the cross-examination of a male defendant, and lawyers were likely to lead unsophisticated and uneducated men into indiscreet admissions.

The defendant's case was less predictable than the plaintiff's, depending whether he denied any breach; acknowledged it and tried to influence the jury towards low damages; or, as occasionally happened, pulled the rabbit from the hat with an irrefutable defence. In 1891, *The Guardian* spared the blushes of an unnamed plaintiff when the defendant produced a letter in which she expressed her pleasure in breaking the engagement and stated that her decision was irrevocable. It was not unusual for a defendant to have no witnesses to confirm his story and to rely solely on the impression his barrister could create.

***

Act Three was the summing up, with each barrister emphasising the justice of their client's case. The plaintiff's barrister trusted that the jury would do the right thing by awarding his client exemplary damages, whilst the defendant's often pointed out that the plaintiff had had a lucky escape by not marrying the defendant and that low damages would meet the justice of the case. Occasionally, an advocate could push the theatrical too far, and at the Liverpool Assizes of spring 1849, Sergeant Wilkins serenaded the audience with a parody of the Irish folk-song, *Molly Malone*. The impromptu performance reduced those present to gales of laughter and the judge had to warn the jury not to be led away from the facts of the case by the humorous speech of the defendant's counsel.

When both sides had concluded their case, the judge, himself a trained lawyer who had practised as a barrister, had to sum up the arguments for the jury. This involved identifying the salient facts, advising the jury of the law, and offering guidance about what jurors should take into consideration in determining damages if they found for the plaintiff. Judges were supposed to be objective, but in many cases they tried to steer the jury towards a verdict for the plaintiff. The majority of judges supported the breach of promise claim because it deterred men from lying to women about their intentions, but a few were opposed to it unless the woman had sustained identifiable harm.

Judges usually summed up fairly, but their personal views can sometimes be detected in their approach and emphasis. They tended to point out that a woman suffered substantial detriment to her prospects in life when a man broke their engagement. In some cases where there was negligible evidence of a promise of marriage the judge refrained from telling the jury what constituted evidence and said that they would have to decide whether they thought there was a promise or not. Very occasionally, a strict judge reminded jurors that a serious offer of marriage and a definite acceptance were fundamental aspects of the law.

The final scene of the courtroom drama was left to the jury who, as men without any legal training, represented the prevailing views of male, middle-class society. The majority of breach of promise cases were decided by a Common Jury of men whose property reached a particular rateable value, usually lower-middle class men running their own small businesses. Women whose property met the rateable value were not eligible to be jurors until 1921. Either party to a claim could request that the case was heard by a Special Jury, for which privilege they had to pay a small fee. A Special Jury consisted of men whose property had a higher rateable value, those in reputable professions or who were titled. Electing for trial by a Special Jury meant that those of higher social standing could guarantee being judged by their social equals.

The female plaintiff, rather than the facts, was usually the most important consideration for jurors, and barristers accentuated a woman's feminine qualities. Men and women were believed to have separate but complementary roles, and as novelist Anthony Trollope explained, 'a woman's life is not perfect or whole till she has added herself to a husband. Nor is a man's life perfect or whole till he has added to himself a wife'. To the class of men who made up a jury, women were seen, not necessarily as an inferior sex, but as a weaker one needing special consideration. A man who reneged on his duty to protect and provide when he had secured a dependant woman's heart, broke a social taboo, whatever his reasons for deciding to end the engagement. If the judge indicated that the scoundrel had also reduced her chances of finding someone else who would marry her, jurors saw this as a very serious injury.

In breach of promise cases, jurors sometimes returned improbable verdicts for the plaintiff which were not supported by the evidence, or awarded disproportionately high damages. On several occasions when a judge guided jurors to a verdict for the defendant or low damages, juries responded with a verdict for the plaintiff and an award of a few hundred pounds. Humanitarian impulses came to the fore and some jurors were prepared to redistribute capital from a man with means to a woman who had little money of her own to give her more economic independence. Even if an engagement had been of very short duration, poor women would have been sorely vexed by loss of the security marriage could provide. Those who had been engaged for a few years had voluntarily given up the possibility of finding another suitor who would have supported them.

Where middle-class juries particularly lacked judgement was when dealing with working-class defendants, as they seem to have had little appreciation of how much a poor man could afford, or what his former fiancée had lost. Some juries rewarded impudent claims with considerable damages and failed to draw an appropriate line between ensuring a poor woman obtained her legal costs and condoning those who were exploiting vulnerable men.

Contemporaries also regularly criticised jurors for basing damages on a woman's looks and there is evidence in newspaper reports of attractive women who received substantial awards. Significantly, some women whose claims were dismissed by juries, or who received trivial or contemptuous damages to compensate them for the property stolen by their fiancé, appear to have been plain, or otherwise figures of fun. That such decisions were not publicly criticised shows a very ugly side to Victorian society, underneath its respectable middle-class façade.

Newspapers regularly reported the reaction of the crowd to the verdict and damages. This was usually cheering, but particularly generous awards gave rise to gasps of surprise and unexpectedly low ones to shock. Very occasionally the reaction of a defendant to a favourable verdict was reported. In 1817, Mr Dennis and his friends paraded around Cambridge with knots of ribbons in their hats, whilst in 1828, 'Mr Joseph Acres, the defendant, was seen riding out of Hertford in a right merry mood, with a streaming bunch of yellow ribbons in his hat, and followed by a crowd of shouting townspeople'. More usually the final glimpse of a defendant reveals him sitting morosely as his barrister asks for the payment of the damages to be delayed so that an appeal could be made.

Decisions in Assize Courts were not the end of the case, as the jury's verdict had to be recorded at the Royal Courts of Justice in London. If the plaintiff or defendant was unhappy with the outcome this could be raised, possibly leading to a further set of hearings before judges in which the parties could argue whether the jury's verdict should be set aside and a new trial granted. It was extremely rare for the jury's decision, however absurd, not to be upheld, as is shown by the claim of Bessie Jones which was heard in 1882. The presiding judge refused to accept the jury's verdict of £150 damages, because her evidence was full of contradiction and inconsistency, whilst Thomas Greenwood's story was much more credible. Despite his disquiet, senior judges in the Royal Courts of Justice decided to enter the verdict, stating that the jury must have taken all of this into consideration when finding for the plaintiff.

Appeal against a verdict was possible on a point of law, or sometimes on a point of fact. Making successful appeal against a disproportionate award of damages was almost impossible unless the plaintiff had maliciously overstated the defendant's wealth. The consistent refusal of senior judges to intervene in cases where the damages were very disproportionate to the defendant's means does them little credit. Their failure to ensure that damages were realistic contributed to the growing criticism of breach of promise as an unfair claim and indicates that judges were out of touch with the lower classes.

After a verdict had been entered a formal appeal could then be made to a higher court. This was the Exchequer Chamber until 1875, when a new Court of Appeal was set up, staffed by very experienced judges. For the next 80 years, the Appeal Court found itself determining a number of technical matters arising from broken engagements, including the ownership of the engagement ring, the rights of those involved in bigamous unions and whether promises to marry were valid if they involved people who were in the process of divorce.

Newspaper reports reveal how much public interest in breach

of promise cases changed over time. After 1830, the Assizes gradually disappeared as informal holidays because industrial and commercial development drew people into a defined employment with fixed hours. By the 1860s those jostling in court for space were probably from the unemployed working-class. In 1869, *The Times* recorded, 'as is usual in cases of this description the details were received with bursts of laughter from the crowd of idlers who block up every passage in this miserable court'.

Rigid, if unwritten, codes of social respectability developed and middle-class ladies were rarely seen at court hearings. Middle-class men and those aspiring to upward mobility, may have thought twice before entering a court-room to be entertained by scandal. Interest had not completely disappeared, as was demonstrated in 1884 when actress May Finney sued Lord Garmoyle, the son of an Earl. This was the first high profile breach of promise trial for some years and public interest far exceeded the capacity of the small London courtroom. Leaders of fashionable society and stage celebrities were spotted in the audience. Women were accommodated on the jurors' benches, forcing the jurors to struggle into court through a door at the back of the jury box and stand closely packed together. Presumably they were delighted when counsel opened the hearing by announcing that the claim had been settled.

The content of breach of promise cases after 1850 would have been less entertaining to an audience. As middle-class ladies abandoned court hearings in favour of private arrangements, the likelihood of high damages was reduced. After 1869, when it became impossible to infer an engagement, reading from a defendant's letters was less common, reducing the titillation that many in the public gallery craved. The mundane problems of working-class plaintiffs would have held little interest for their contemporaries.

Theatre now provided a new, and respectable, way to be entertained by breach of promise. In 1875, *Trial by Jury* became the first of Gilbert and Sullivan's many light-hearted musical comedies. The plot is based on contemporary expectations of a breach of promise trial; a beautiful, amoral and supposedly heartbroken plaintiff, a hapless defendant, avaricious attorneys and the sort of neat ending that could not be guaranteed by the real thing;

the judge solving everyone's dilemma by deciding to marry the plaintiff himself. Music Hall was more working-class than the theatre and by the 1870s it was reflecting the trials and tribulations of working-class plaintiffs in a range of saucy situations, replicating the vicarious thrills that had once stemmed from the reading of letters. It reached its triumphant peak in 1907 with *Waiting at the Church*, one of the most famous Music Hall routines of all time, in which a naïve woman cheerily explains how she has been tricked out of her savings by the lies of a married man.

The transfer of breach of promise from the confined courtroom to the public auditorium confirms that until the Great War, a broken engagement was not viewed as a private tragedy but as public property. The parallels between court hearings and public theatre capture one very unpleasant aspect of broken engagements in the nineteenth century; the willingness of all sections of society to find amusement in the misfortunes of others.

Chapter 5

ESCAPING FROM THE SPIDER'S WEB
DEFENCES TO CLAIMS FOR BREACH OF PROMISE

*I have no wish to grieve you but I don't wish to take you into a
circle that will look upon you with ridicule.*
(Michael Bright, *The Guardian*, 13 March 1866)

From the instant a woman received his offer of marriage a man
was caught in a trap. Even if he regretted his folly as soon as the
words left his mouth, there was no escape unless his beloved
released him from his promise. It is likely that several thousand
men discreetly bought their way out of an unwise proposal. If a
man was not prepared to make a woman his wife and she was
not prepared to accept his offer of financial recompense, the only
option was a day in court whilst a jury decided how much money
the jilted bride deserved for her blighted hopes. Breach of promise
claims could bring out the worst in both parties and court hearings
often highlighted to everyone present just how fortunate it was
that the marriage had not gone ahead.

Before a case found its way into the courtroom lawyers would
try to forge a settlement between the couple, but some offers of
amends were too trivial to be taken seriously. In 1866, wealthy
Michael Bright offered a paltry £20 to Annie Thorpe to return his
letters and presents of jewellery. In court, the jury was infuriated
by his comments about Annie's low social status and awarded her
£500. Several women had unrealistic hopes of how much money
a court would give them. Others were intent on shaming the man
in public and were not the injured innocents portrayed by their
barristers. A few women had a reason other than money for having
the claim heard. Women working as governesses and companions
sometimes needed to prove their good character, by showing that
they had given the man no grounds to break the engagement, in

order to protect their future employment prospects.

Faced with the inevitability of a court hearing, a defendant had four options: he could claim that he lacked the legal capacity to enter into an engagement; admit that he had broken the engagement and try to mitigate the damages; deny that the couple were engaged; or argue that he was justified in refusing to marry the plaintiff. These lines of defence were not mutually exclusive and it was not unusual for the defendant to deny the existence of an engagement, state that the plaintiff had released him from his obligations and also put forward his reasons for breaking it. When a man successfully defended a claim it is not always apparent which of his many contentions had influenced the jury in his favour.

Defences based on the man's legal capacity to form an engagement arose from contract law and related to the defendant's level of understanding when he offered marriage. Contract law deemed that anyone under 21 had insufficient understanding to enter into a binding agreement and allowed the minor to walk away from their promise if they wished. Cases involving the defence of age were hardly ever heard by a jury, as someone's date of birth was a matter of fact and not usually difficult to establish. Whether the plaintiff knew the man's age when she accepted the proposal was irrelevant. If the man chose not to renew it when he reached his majority, then the woman had no grounds to bring a claim.

Not understanding the implications of a proposal or being unaware of making one were valid defences only when a man had a severe mental illness or a condition that would now be described as a severe learning disability, or if he had been so drunk that he had no idea what he was saying when he mentioned marriage. In practice, these points were rarely argued before a jury as clinical knowledge was low and expert witnesses were not abundant. Until the late nineteenth century, the law was more concerned about the plaintiff's blighted hopes than the defendant's impaired understanding. In 1801, Miss Vaughan was awarded the verdict against 75-year-old dementia sufferer Mr Albridge in a case the jurors were clearly uncomfortable with. The damages of £10 were derisory and the verdict appears to have been motivated by which party would pay the legal costs.

In 1896, Annie Sealy sued Devonshire solicitor William Creed. He had been compulsorily admitted to an asylum just after he made Annie a written offer of marriage. Creed went into the witness box and swore that he had no memory of several points in her evidence, including writing the letter containing his promise to marry her. Annie lost her claim because Creed could not remember what he had done during his illness. Defendants who became insane after making a proposal were held liable for damages and those with episodic mental illness also had to pay to escape the engagement if their symptoms had not been acute when the offer was made.

In the nineteenth century, men who had learning disabilities were considered to be responsible for their proposals, though juries might award trivial damages to a calculating woman. In 1893, Lucy Shepherd received only a farthing from her employer's brother, Frederick White, an elderly and simple-minded man who was 40 years older than the enterprising housemaid. After rejecting one proposal she brought a ring for him to give her when he mentioned marriage again. Awarding a verdict against a vulnerable man, even if it was negated by a small award of damages, made this group of people more vulnerable to exploitation, as some families would settle a claim rather than help their relative to defend it.

Drunkenness was regarded as a form of mental illness but it was a difficult defence to succeed with. Men whose tongues were loosened by a few drinks were not considered to lack capacity and had to suffer the consequences of raising the woman's hopes, even for a short period of time. Chronic alcoholics, and men who were very inebriated when they proposed, usually managed to escape from their promise if the woman had deliberately taken advantage of words uttered without understanding. This was normally reflected in an award of low damages rather than a successful defence of the claim.

***

In contrast to the small number of defendants who argued their lack of capacity to enter into a valid engagement or marriage, around 50 per cent of defendants offered no defence at all and acknowledged breaking the engagement. Not all men did so willingly. Poorer men had to keep the legal costs as low as possible and one way was to hand victory to the woman and hope that the jury would not ruin him when compensating her. Sensible men explained their reasons for breaking the engagement temperately and offered no criticism of the woman.

In legal terms there was no difference between a woman who had lost little from the broken engagement and one who had suffered great harm, but juries were sometimes pragmatic on this point when a man's change of mind arose from a change in his circumstances and not from a selfish whim. In 1875, a sympathetic judge summing up at Monmouth Assizes emphasised that William Haines had not been unreasonable in refusing to marry when his health began to fail and told the jury to consider this when assessing the injury to Margaret Williams's feelings.

An occasional man may have had his own reasons for not defending a case. Limiting the collateral damage of wide press coverage may explain why Harcourt Master, a married man with a young family, did not defend actress Carlotta Huntly's claim in 1896. The day after the hearing, Caroline Master noticed whilst having breakfast that a portion of the daily newspaper had been torn off. When Master left for work, she fetched another copy and discovered that her philandering husband had pretended to be single to seduce the actress and then lied about moving to Africa when he decided to abandon her. Four months later, Caroline cited this to support her successful request for a judicial separation.

For men like Harcourt Master, who possessed little sense or scruple, the law offered a tantalising opportunity to escape their engagement without having to pay a penny, if they could prove that certain circumstances applied. Men with low moral standards were prepared to argue, with varying degrees of ingenuity, that their situation fell into one of those categories. To a modern eye, some of their contentions appear ludicrous. A few would also have appeared so to contemporaries, but many were rooted in the values of their age. For defendants to put forward any argument indicates a hope that it would find favour with the men who sat in the jury box. Most defendants were represented by experienced lawyers who understood what might just, and what definitely would not, sway a jury in their client's favour.

Two arguments became known as the standard defences. These were that there had never been a promise of marriage or, if there had been such a promise, the parties had released each other from their obligations. It was not always easy to determine when a courtship became an engagement and the way a couple behaved towards each other, or were regarded by other people, could be used as evidence of their intention to wed. Sometimes a woman's family or friends colluded by pretending that the defendant had spoken of marriage or plied him with drink until he actually did so.

After the Evidence (Further) Amendment Act of 1869 raised the standard of proof required, it became easier for a man to deny that marriage had been offered, although juries were not easy to convince on this point. A few defendants appealed successfully on the basis that there was inadequate confirmation of a promise of marriage, after failing to persuade a lay jury that a promise had never been uttered.

It was unusual for a man to convince a jury that a couple had agreed to end their engagement. The notion that a woman would willingly free a man and risk remaining a spinster was difficult to comprehend in a society that perceived a woman's true purpose in life was as a wife and mother. In 1860, when Thomas Bomford alleged that Fanny Davies had released him from his promise almost everyone in the Worcester courtroom expressed surprise that his word was believed instead of hers. It is possible that the jury found the idea of a woman enriching herself more than once with damages for breach of promise unacceptable, as Fanny had received £54 from a Mr Skinner by agreement a year earlier.

Mimicking the requirement for sufficient proof of a promise of marriage, juries usually required strong confirmation that a woman had agreed to end her engagement before they found for the man. In 1876, this led a Bury alderman, George Yates, to deceive Betsy Barlow into signing a receipt for £100 in full settlement of her claim against him. Betsy explained that when she signed the paper it contained much less writing and related to a different debt. In 1880, John Wootton argued that as Anna Palmer had given birth to a child by another man in 1876, she must have considered their own youthful engagement had ended by this date. Mr Justice Bramwell, hearing her claim at the Norfolk Assizes, described it as the most impudent action he had ever heard of.

In the eighteenth and nineteenth centuries, engagements were sometimes entered into with conditions attached by one or both parties. The bride's age at marriage was one consideration for her parents. Queen Victoria's eldest daughter was engaged at 14, on the understanding that her wedding would not take place for another three years. Another condition often imposed was that satisfactory enquiries were made into the background and finances of the suitor. This reflected the social and economic mobility brought about by the Industrial Revolution. It was more necessary when the man was a stranger to the area than when he was from a local and well-established family.

Some conditional engagements were made with no marriage date in mind. One practical problem for men contemplating marriage was the Poor Law which obliged children to maintain parents unable to support themselves, so that indigent, elderly people did not become a burden on the ratepayers of the parish. For a young man providing for a widowed mother or an unmarried sister, it was impossible to estimate when he might be able to afford a wife and family.

To a young woman, an open-ended engagement was not necessarily undesirable, as someone who was 'spoken for' enjoyed a respect that an unattached spinster did not. She could assist in running the family home, caring for older relatives, helping with younger siblings or in the family trade or business, or possibly doing a bit of sewing on her own account to save some money for married life. Her relatives knew that at some point her fiancé would take responsibility for her living costs, or if he did not then a claim for breach of promise could be made. To protect themselves from this eventuality, astute men placed a limit on the time it might take them to acquire the means to support a wife. If the marriage did not take place within that period, both parties became free from their obligations. It was practical, if unromantic.

There was no particular level of income that determined when a marriage was affordable; everything depended on the needs and aspirations of the couple. Jane Austen revealed that neither Elinor Dashwood nor Edward Ferrars, a genteel, upper-middle-class couple contemplating marriage in 1811, were quite enough in love to think that £350 a year would supply them with the comforts of life. A claim brought in 1886, by governess Elizabeth Myers against an Islington dental assistant revealed that, for a couple with pretensions of gentility, marriage was likely to be a miserable experience for both if their income was less than £150 a year. This equated to £3 (60 shillings) a week.

A review of *The Times* in 1886 demonstrates this. Rented accommodation for a married couple cost around 10 shillings a week. Furniture was available on hire purchase but, with a piano costing four shillings a week over three years, this type of refinement was unaffordable if a bed, lounge furniture and kitchen equipment were also needed. Food could cost around 20 shillings each week. Coal for cooking and heating cost around five shillings a week depending on the time of year. The couple would need clothes and the man might have to travel to work by public transport, swallowing up a few more shillings over the working week. With theatre seats costing one shilling, entertainment would be a rarity and help with domestic chores an unaffordable luxury, obliging the woman to do all the shopping, cooking, cleaning, washing and mending herself. If children came along the extra cost would be very hard to absorb.

Conditional engagements began with a young man's honest intention to work diligently and earn the money to marry his sweetheart. Geographic mobility was common amongst men aspiring to a career in a retail, commercial or professional establishment and some moved many miles away to find employment. Respectable lodgings for single men cost around 40 shillings a week, if meals and laundry were provided. Accommodation, food and the necessary incidental costs of working might swallow the majority of the weekly wage, making it hard to accumulate savings quickly and set up a marital home without help from the family or an inheritance. If the young couple did not see each other regularly there was a strong probability that they would grow apart, especially if they had not known each other for very long.

Distant courtships might be sustained by letter for a few years, though if one or both parties could not write, even this limited form of contact could not maintain the affection between them. It was usual for couples to write to each other several times a week and when Kate Lamb sued Arthur Fryer, her barrister produced more than 900 letters written almost daily by the pair over 18 months and stated their total length as 2 and three quarter miles. In court, the man's correspondence was usually described as profuse and affectionate after the initial parting, but then gradually petering out. Later letters usually contained stilted assurances that the man still loved the woman and intended to make her his wife, clearly answering reproaches and uncertainties raised in her letters to him. At some point the relationship ended when the man finally failed to reply to her letters.

In November 1886, the *Girl's Own Paper* described how close friendships formed between young women at finishing school withered away in nine out of ten cases. Letters became shorter and fewer as the distant friends developed new lives and interests and struggled in fitful correspondence to find meaningful topics to write about. The paper advised that when the kernel of a once-strong relationship had gone, it was better to fling away the empty husk and make new friends with people who were available to provide companionship than cling on to the past. Ironically, when the fitful correspondence was between a young man and woman who had become strangers, the man was castigated as heartless and cruel. In breach of promise cases he could be ordered to pay a couple of hundred pounds damages if he concluded that he and his former love now had so little in common that marriage would be foolhardy.

Conditional, open-ended engagements were rooted in aspiration and fantasy. They could unrealistically raise a woman's hopes and placed a heavy burden on a man to honour an idealistic commitment made when he was young and without much experience of life. History only reveals the women who were successful in court. It leaves no trace of those who consulted a solicitor only to find that they could not prove the promise; those whose courtship never turned into a formal engagement, those who were unable to locate a missing fiancé in order to sue him or who refused other opportunities out of misplaced loyalty. In the twentieth century public opinion turned against long engagements and women were criticised for deluding themselves that marriage lay ahead. Men were no longer held responsible for wasting the best years of a woman's life; she was considered to have done that herself.

Faced with a court hearing, men sometimes argued that the conditions attached to an engagement had not been fulfilled, though if a man had married someone else, the law considered that he had broken his promise at that point, whether the stipulated condition had been met or not. Taking a wife made it impossible for him to honour the commitment to his first love.

Some conditional promises were based on the mercenary consideration that an inheritance would provide the funds to support the couple. How long a father in good health would remain alive was unknown and expectations from a bachelor uncle could evaporate in an instant if he decided to marry, or changed his will. It seems likely that some men who based their promise on the expectation of an inheritance were not completely sincere. An unusual breach of a conditional promise was Edward Paty's refusal in 1887 to marry Jane Green. Their engagement was based on Jane's expectations from her grandfather. When he died without leaving anything to her, Paty considered that his £70 annual salary was too small to support a wife. The jury decided that, whether he could afford a wife or not, he should pay Jane £100 for reneging on his commitment.

When an inheritance was involved, the man was often of a higher social rank and most women appear unwise in placing any trust in the proposal. Marriages where a woman moved into a significantly higher social class were unusual, unless her father had made money in a trade and could provide her with a good marriage settlement. Even when the man remained loyal, family opposition to a son marrying a poor girl could prove insurmountable. James Rollinson's love for Margaret Turner, one of the family servants, incensed his father who stated in his will that James would forfeit the ancestral estate in Cumberland if the couple ever wed.

Between 1815 and 1818, a poor farmer's daughter, Esther Dawson, refused at least four offers of marriage, including one from Jonas Hayward who had £500, a good suitor for a girl of such limited means. Esther believed she was engaged to Isaac

Newton, the son of a wealthy landowner, who lived at Foulstone near Huddersfield. Growing up a mile apart, the pair had known each other from childhood and affection appears to have existed on both sides. Nelson was a regular visitor to her parents' cottage and gave Esther an engagement ring and a silk dress for their wedding, which was to take place when his father died and he inherited an estate producing income of £20,000 a year. In spring 1818, Nelson abandoned her in favour of heiress Hannah Dunn from Howden, a more suitable match for a landowner's son.

In 1819, Esther went to court. Nelson's barrister attacked her character, arguing that she could not rely on bantering promises that his client had made in public houses, and at fairs and wakes. He asked whether it was likely that a man of Nelson's social standing would wish to marry a part-time barmaid. Although her morals were denigrated by Nelson, who was described in newspaper reports as 'a fat, stout, coarse-looking man', the testimony of his witnesses on this point served only to prove that Esther, described in the same papers as 'handsome, modest and interesting', was a very principled woman. She was awarded £300. The following year, she attracted a sixth proposal and married Peter Haigh, a local man. She spent the rest of her life in Holmfirth with her husband and children. It was not the wealthy lifestyle she had once been promised, but it was a realistic one for the daughter of a tenant farmer. Whether she would have been happier with Jonas Hayward or any of her other rejected suitors is an intriguing unknown.

A small number of breach of promise claims were defended with the contention that one of the couple was too ill for married life. If, after promises to marry had been exchanged, the health of one party deteriorated substantially, the other could break the engagement with impunity. The sick person occasionally managed to escape an engagement using this defence, until 1857 when a landmark case confirmed that a person could not rely on their own weakness to evade a promise. George Wright said that it would be dangerous for him to marry Isabella Hall because he was too frail to fulfil the duties of marriage without risk to his life. Recognising that a legal point was involved, the judge asked the jury to decide whether they accepted Wright's contention and if they did, to state what damages they would have awarded if they had found that Isabella had been jilted without a proper reason.

The jurors initially found for Wright but Isabella tenaciously pursued a series of appeals in every possible court until the judges of the Exchequer Court, the final possible arbiter, decided by a slim majority that Wright's inability to carry out the duties of marriage did not dissolve his contract. In 1859, coachman's daughter Isabella finally collected the £100 that the original jury would have awarded had it upheld her claim.

This case restricted a plea of ill-health to mitigating the damages rather than providing an absolute defence, but jurors continued to struggle when a man's health was involved. In 1868, the London jury considering Dora Otte's claim against Ronald Grant was discharged when it was unable to decide whether Grant had acted reasonably by asking Dora to defer their wedding until his health improved. Two years in India had left him 'a mere bag of bones'. The question was not put to a second jury as Dora found a new suitor and married him a few months later.

It took until 1920 before men with serious health problems received some protection from being sued for breach of promise. In March that year, Mr Justice Darling, who was determining a claim without a jury, awarded a contemptuous farthing to Caroline Gamble. She had sued a shell-shocked and war-wounded soldier, William Sales, who argued that he was too weak and nervous to marry and that it was against public policy to force him to. In reasoning that now makes uncomfortable reading, the judge supported the view that children born to a man in the defendant's condition were likely to be 'practically useless' and 'a burden on the state'.

Given this decision, it is surprising that later in the year, four days after the burial of the Unknown Soldier and the unveiling of the cenotaph had honoured all those who died in the Great War, a London jury awarded Louise Savage £500 from Charles Thacker, a 30-year-old war veteran decorated with the military cross. Thacker explained that recent surgery left him unfit to contemplate marriage. Louise argued that it was a woman's prerogative to decide whether her fiancé's health was an obstacle for her. In its short report of the case, *The Guardian* focussed on the jury's disapproval of Thacker's selfish and unmanly decision to break the engagement. *The Times* covered the case in more depth and the tremors of shell-shock reverberate through Thacker's defence like the pounding of heavy artillery. To a modern reader it seems indisputable that a serious operation proved the final straw for a brave and decent man whose nerves had been stretched to breaking point by bullets and mustard gas in the trenches.

Patrick Scanlon was also held responsible for being too weak to rise above an external event that had changed his life. He received no sympathy from a Lancashire jury in 1934 when he explained that after a motor accident his whole outlook changed and he did not think it was right for him to form a union with anyone. Press coverage hints that his fiancee's mother thought the accident had perceptibly affected his health. Advances in knowledge about psychological trauma suggest that Scanlon and Thacker each had good insight into their fragile mental condition. Better public understanding of the subject would probably have resulted in different verdicts. There were no cases of women refusing to marry men who developed psychological illnesses, so the law did not have to decide whether their refusal was reasonable.

A feature of breach of promise cases is that a successful argument in one immediately led to copy-cat reasoning in another. Shortly after George Wright's initial victory about his own health, Frederick Rosenberg, a Manchester tobacconist, alleged that Estelle Abrahams was too frail for marriage, as he needed a strong, healthy woman to help him with the business. Rosenberg lost the case because the jury did not accept his contention that Estelle was ill. Although Rosenberg might appear heartless, a woman's state of health could be a major consideration when making a proposal. Working men sometimes selected a wife not for love or affection, but to provide help in earning a livelihood. Running a shop entailed hard physical work moving stock, and long hours standing up to serve customers. If a wife's delicate health meant hiring assistance in the shop or a servant to help in the house this could be the difference between making a living and scraping an existence.

The few men who contended that their fiancée was unsuitable for marriage because of her poor health usually stated or hinted that she had tuberculosis, also known until the 1850s as consumption. Tuberculosis is a contagious bacterial infection which often attacks and damages the lungs and leads to symptoms such as coughing up blood, loss of appetite and weight, night sweats and fever. Until the discovery of antibiotics there was no effective treatment or cure. Sufferers were advised to live a quiet lifestyle and to rest as much as possible.

Although the defence that a woman was ill proved unsuccessful in the nineteenth and twentieth century courts and usually resulted in exemplary damages for the woman because of the serious accusation made against her, it generally failed because the man could provide no evidence for his claim. A woman was not obliged to submit to an independent medical examination and generally provided a statement from her own physician that her health was sound. It is unclear whether a jury would have accepted a woman's ill-health as a valid reason to end an engagement if the man had been able to prove it.

A man who could not deny an engagement sometimes resorted to the high-risk strategy of arguing that he had discovered the plaintiff had a bad character; entitling him to withdraw the offer of marriage he had made in the belief that she was a virtuous woman. If he succeeded then he paid no damages, but if he could not provide evidence of his allegation the woman usually obtained a much higher award of damages than she might have anticipated. Despite the risks, around five per cent of defendants were prepared to take a chance, though usually with a woman from a lower social class than their own.

Bad character was usually synonymous with sexual impropriety with a man other than the defendant. One of the very few men to succeed was Samuel Brighouse, an elderly gentleman who was conned into proposing to Betty Wadsworth, a weaver with low morals, in 1872. She lived nearby and appeared to him as a respectable young woman. Her barrister stated her case, called her to give evidence and then squirmed with embarrassment as she refused to answer any questions from Brighouse's barrister about her relationships with other men. After the judge threatened Betty with prison unless she answered the questions, her barrister withdrew his services as her advocate and her claim collapsed.

A man who wanted to walk away from a promise of marriage because of a woman's bad character had to convince a jury that he was not aware of it when proposing and had not confirmed his promise after he found out. It was conventional for a woman who had a dubious episode hidden in her past to reveal it in confidence after receiving a proposal. If the man did not withdraw his offer immediately, then he was unable to plead bad character to justify a later change of mind. This was a reasonable approach, as most defences alleging a woman's bad character arose because the man had a different reason for wishing to end the engagement.

A woman's sexual immorality could not be offered as a defence by a man who had been her lover, unless she had concealed from him similar conduct with another man. Around 1820, a short-lived, and unsuccessful, line of reasoning developed that if a woman allowed herself to be seduced by the man she was engaged to, then she did not value her virtue. When this happened, the man should be entitled to rescind the offer of marriage as he could not trust her to respect her marriage vows. In 1884, the defence of bad character became much more restricted when Henry Smith, a Fulham publican who had cohabited with widowed Helen McHale, was not allowed to rely on his recent discovery that her children were illegitimate to justify leaving her for someone else.

As the scope for a defence of bad character narrowed, lawyers rediscovered an argument used early in the nineteenth century. Their clients began to contend that the woman had chosen to live as a mistress without any expectation of marriage. This proved a very effective means of walking away from an engagement, as it removed all onus from the man to prove bad character and placed the burden on the woman to prove a promise of marriage. It was a barrier that working-class women struggled to clear.

Occasionally men identified bad character in other aspects of conduct. More than one asked an incredulous jury to believe that the woman was a drunkard who imbibed in secret, unknown to anyone else in the house, from hidden supplies purchased anonymously. When Richard Woosnam accused Emma Partridge of drinking nine glasses of alcohol on a day out in Epping Forest, the jury awarded her £500. The foreman of the jury stated that Emma left court without a stain on her character as the allegations against her were totally unfounded.

Bad character brought a few absurd contentions into the

courtroom, displaying immaturity, lack of judgement or social snobbery. In 1837, an attempt to prove that a young Somerset dressmaker, Mary Ann Hunt, had a bad character rebounded on William Chick after he broke their engagement and married Betsy Rason. Chick anxiously confided to Abraham Stoodleigh that Mary Ann would be given half his property unless he could prove that he was justified in leaving her. He offered 10 shillings to any local man prepared to stand up in court and declare that Mary Ann was a common prostitute. Stoodleigh declined the money, told Mary Ann of the plot and appeared as her witness instead. She was awarded £300, a third of the capital Chick had recently inherited on his twenty-first birthday.

In 1877, Cambridge undergraduate Harry Crotton regretting his hasty proposal to rector's daughter, Mary May, told her family that she was untruthful. Pressed to be specific about her lies, Crotton said that she once described travelling in a carriage with her brother from Bath to Devizes. The truth was that they only travelled together from Trowbridge, as her brother rode the first part of the journey in a different carriage. The allegation proved catastrophic for Crotton as the May family would have accepted the broken engagement if the accusation of lying had not been made. He was ordered to pay Mary £1,000 in damages, and was fortunate to negotiate a reduction following an appeal.

Joseph Joplin, a 28-year-old wine and spirit merchant from Liverpool, tried to justify ending his engagement to Georgiana Reeves in 1867 because she was illegitimate. This was not regarded as proof of bad character, and her guardian also gave evidence that Joplin knew this when he proposed. He was not the only man to cite illegitimacy as a stigma, but he was from a lower social class than others who raised the point, indicating how the tightening morality of the Victorian period was penetrating down the social scale.

For William Brenton, a doctor with a large practice in Plymouth, snobbery proved an insuperable barrier to his marriage with a nurse in 1896. He broke his engagement to Mary Maunder, alleging that she had misled him about her social standing by speaking about her father as though he were a man of means and pretending that she worked for interest rather than to earn a living. Mary denied that she had ever deceived the doctor about her family's income or her father's work as a parish verger. The jury decided that Brenton's mistake about the lowly social standing of his fiancée, or his belief that she was a social-climber, did not justify him breaking his promise to marry her.

Incompatibility and falling out of love were never defences to a breach of promise claim, even as the belief grew that marriage should be based on love and affection. Breach of promise law rigidly regarded one party as injured and the other as at fault, though several engagements floundered because of problems on both sides. In nineteenth century Britain a large number of religious sects and beliefs jockeyed for supremacy and souls, and differences of outlook or belief caused irreconcilable problems for Catholic and Protestant, Christadelphian and Spiritualist, Quaker and Methodist, Christian and Jew.

Even between apparently well-matched couples, differences in personality or values could emerge. In 1858, after a three-year engagement, Richard Stirzaker, a market gardener from Lancaster, and Elizabeth Ridley quarrelled a few weeks before their wedding. Needing a personal maid for her new home, Elizabeth appointed a very reliable woman on a salary of £12 a year without consulting her fiancé. Scandalised, Richard told her that a servant could be hired for £9 and that he could not afford such extravagance. Elizabeth dismissed the unfortunate woman and told her husband-to-be that she would leave him the pleasure of appointing a good quality servant for her. Richard found her attitude saucy, sarcastic, and insulting and he suddenly realised that Elizabeth was not the woman he wished to spend his life with but proud and haughty; unlikely to make him a fit wife and create a comfortable home.

In the nineteenth century, breach of promise law ignored the role of the plaintiff when an engagement broke down and considered that a woman's poor conduct was not a reason to reduce her damages. Any man who drew attention to unreasonable behaviour by a woman risked an exemplary award of damages against him. It seems possible that Catherine Knights of London charmed landowner Samuel Thistlewood into a proposal in 1861 and then behaved in a deliberately disrespectful manner until she managed to provoke him into calling off the wedding. She then succeeded in winning £600 damages for his broken promise and married someone else a few months later.

By the early twentieth century, juries refused to be liberal with damages when the woman's conduct had caused or contributed to the break. This became clear in 1914 when Elsie Lummis received one farthing from John Taylor, whose change of mind arose from her repeated outbursts of temper. Unsurprisingly, others copied the defence. Later that year, Herbert Zeal walked out on Florence Oxley after she spent an evening finding fault with him. In court Zeal said that Florence could be bad-tempered, though this was not deemed sufficient reason to avoid paying her £75. The different approach of the two juries probably reflected the fact that Taylor had discussed Elsie's temper with her several times before and given her opportunities to control her tantrums.

From the 1920s, defences to breach of promise claims became temperate, if pointed, arguments about whether there had been a valid promise of marriage, occasionally going through the legal system and to the House of Lords for decisions on points of law. The harsh attitude of judges and juries towards fanciful defences, vindictive claims and plaintiffs whose own conduct contributed to the breach meant that the parties found it in their interest to resolve any differences by negotiation and the number of cases reaching court was reduced to a handful.

Defences to breach of promise claims ranged from fair and honest to implausible and insulting. In their inventiveness, men who tried to walk away from their obligations without making proper recompense were no more outrageous than women who lied about proposals or schemed to entrap. Around a tenth of cases reaching the courtroom were defended successfully. In a third of these the woman could not prove that a promise had been made. A sixth were attempted extortion and a similar proportion involved a rescinded promise. Only in six per cent of cases was the man deemed justified in ending the engagement because of the woman's bad character. The remaining claims involved very specific factors, such as the jury failing to reach a verdict or the court not having jurisdiction over a promise made abroad.

Some men appear to have mitigated the damages by a temperate defence presented well. Two per cent of defendants paid only a farthing in damages and a further five per cent may have lost solely because the jury wanted to ensure that the woman was not left to pay the lawyers' bills. Despite criticism of the breach of promise action for bias in favour of women, male defendants with a strong case could escape an engagement without too much hurt to their pockets. Yet a fine judgement was involved between taking a chance with a jury and offering a sufficient sum to avoid this gamble.

Chapter 6

Proverbial for their Extravagance
Damages for Breach of Promise

*Where female affection and confidence have been deliberately
betrayed by a heartless seducer, no fine that can be laid on the
defendant is likely to be too heavy.*
(Editorial, *The Times*), 16 February 1865)

Damages for breach of promise were a sum of money paid to the
plaintiff by the defendant to compensate her for not becoming
his wife. However, it was often difficult to decide exactly what
a plaintiff had lost when an engagement was broken, because
everyone's circumstances were different. Marriage to a landed
gentleman with debts might provide a much worse standard of
living than marriage to a tradesman creating a successful business.
A working-class woman jilted by a rich man lost far more than
a middle-class one who enjoyed a comfortable home with her
parents and had opportunities to meet other men of similar wealth
and status.

In law, a broken promise to marry was a breach of contract.
According to contract law, damages should place the injured party
in the financial position they would have enjoyed if the contract had
been honoured. This involved an objective calculation of an actual
loss, ignoring the reasons for the broken contract, the behaviour of
the plaintiff and defendant, any distress or annoyance and the loss
of alternative opportunities.

Whilst this was a fair approach when business transactions went
wrong, these principles took no account of the nature of a broken
promise of marriage, when a woman's reputation could be harmed
by public rejection. Recognising that a commercial approach failed
to do justice to injuries to reputation and health, juries moved away
from treating damages as a strict matter of contract law. By the

nineteenth century, damages for breach of promise included a moral judgement which took into account conduct and social standing.

As there was no formula to calculate the financial value of a lost marriage, juries used their discretion and awarded whatever lump-sum seemed appropriate in the circumstances. Claims for damages could include quantifiable losses, such as abortive expenses incurred in preparing for the wedding, the marriage settlement that the plaintiff would have received from the defendant, and compensation for wages if a woman had given up her job. In addition, there were less tangible aspects such as the loss of status involved in not becoming the wife of a man of the defendant's social and financial standing, the lost opportunity to become another man's wife and gain her own home, a debased reputation and a wounded spirit. These last, nebulous elements related to the publicity and heartbreak of rejection and, until the twentieth century, were considered the most serious injuries arising from the breach.

In court, barristers usually explained the effect of the broken engagement on the plaintiff. Jilted women were said to have no interest in life. They stopped eating and became thin and their youthful looks and charm vanished almost overnight. Such descriptions were common in cases heard a few months after an engagement ended, but were less frequently heard in claims made when the couple had not been in contact for some time. Studies of the effect of loss on individuals have shown that people pass through four distinct stages; denial, grief, adjustment and recovery. Sadness, poor appetite and loss of interest in the world are acknowledged symptoms of the grief phase and subside over time, as the grieving person adjusts to their new situation. In the early nineteenth century, the symptoms of grief were considered as an emotional and physical illness that a woman would struggle to recover from and one for which she deserved ample compensation, as it had been caused by the defendant's selfish behaviour.

In a breach of promise claim, emotional injury was the trump card. Barristers rarely analysed a claim for damages into separate elements but, through artful rhetoric, whipped-up the emotions of the jury with descriptions of the despicable insult to the feelings and reputation of the fair plaintiff. Jurors were invited to avenge the plaintiff by awarding exemplary damages to show their disgust at the defendant's conduct. The effect of this courtroom bombast was that often, subjective judgements about a woman's emotional pain displaced any rational evaluation of her material loss.

Newspaper reports reveal that many juries came to a decision in a few minutes without leaving the jury box or having a proper discussion. The record for a speedy verdict appears to be held by jurors at the Court of the Queen's Bench in 1841. It took them just one minute to award Miss Faulkener £100. As jury discussions are confidential there is no way of knowing how jurors approached their task, but when they took time to discuss a case the decision often appears to be more reasonable than when they did not.

Until the end of the nineteenth century, received wisdom decreed that emotional injury to a woman required substantial compensation. The idea originated in the eighteenth century and was linked to the contemporary belief that a jilted woman would neither wish to marry, nor find another man prepared to take her as his wife. Jurors often failed to distinguish between a man who had behaved so badly that exemplary damages were warranted and one who had simply concluded that marriage was not a sensible step to take. They regularly compensated a beautiful, broken-hearted woman so amply that damages for breach of promise were widely criticised as 'proverbial for their extravagance'.

In 1882, a young London builder, John Clemence, ended his engagement to Clara Pilbeam a month before their wedding when he discovered that he no longer loved his fiancée and felt it would be 'worse than sin' to marry her knowing this. Her barrister branded the young man's honesty as 'peculiar heartlessness' justifying ample damages. Clara received £1,000, a year's income for Clemence. In contrast, four years later, William Bush, a builder from Essex, had to pay Miss Thompson just £140 when he fell madly in love with someone else.

When a man's only fault was to realise that he had made a mistake in proposing marriage and he conducted himself in a gentlemanly manner towards the woman, judges tried to steer the jury towards a sum which provided fair compensation for the plaintiff without ruining the defendant. For a man of moderate or low means there was a very fine line between an affordable award and one that could push him into penury or bankruptcy. Some judges knew from the divorce and criminal courts that marriage vows grudgingly muttered by a groom threatened with a claim for breach of promise could lead to a far more distressing situation for a woman than a broken engagement.

It was almost impossible to appeal against the damages awarded by a jury. Appeal judges considered that deciding damages was the prerogative of the 12 men sworn to hear the case. Very occasionally, if the plaintiff had deliberately overstated the defendant's wealth, appeal judges substituted a more realistic sum, though they consistently refused to help any defendant who had given the plaintiff an exaggerated account of his means to impress her when they were courting. They only felt comfortable about intervening if the jury had heard false evidence or there had been a defect in procedure and in these rare cases would order a new trial. This did not necessarily improve the defendant's position.

In 1863, a teenage William Clapham celebrated the wedding of The Prince of Wales and Alexandra of Denmark by seducing his childhood playmate, Polly Smith, who became pregnant. In 1868, Polly, a blacksmith's daughter, belatedly obtained £100 for Clapham's breach of promise when he unwisely reiterated his proposal after his twenty-first birthday. He appealed and had the verdict set aside, contending that he was a minor when he made it and also drunk. Polly brought a second case and a more liberal jury awarded her £150.

During the nineteenth century, as juries became ever-more generous, appeal judges were reluctantly pushed into forming a view about whether damages were too high. They decided that it was permissible to order a new trial if a jury had been too liberal. In 1828 property developer Richard Broadbent challenged the £500 awarded to Martha Deany, an inn-keeper's niece, as too generous. Broadbent must have been furious when the Lord Chief Justice decided that he could order a new trial because of the size of the damages, but declined to do so, as Broadbent had unjustifiably attacked Martha's character and conduct during the appeal.

The law offered no guidance about reasonable levels of compensation and judges remained very cautious about overruling a jury, believing that the men who had heard all the details of a case were best-placed to decide what the woman should receive. After 1828 a procession of aggrieved defendants learned that senior judges personally considered the damages too high, but not sufficiently excessive to intervene formally. Judges were more likely to request the parties to negotiate a settlement, perhaps mentioning a figure that they thought would be reasonable. As the century progressed, they became more pro-active, offering the plaintiff the choice of a new trial or agreeing a more realistic sum. They were equally unhelpful to the few plaintiffs who complained of low awards, unless a point of law was involved.

The Appeal Court was finally forced to devise guidelines for damages in 1891, after an outraged judge guided a jury towards damages of £10,000 to punish a wealthy defendant. Senior judges confirmed that punitive damages were not allowed and decided that if damages exceeded the 'outside sum' that a jury might reasonably have given to compensate the plaintiff, then they were too high and could be reduced to that amount. Ironically, by the time the judges tackled this thorny question, excessive damages were almost a thing of the past.

**

Damages can neither be understood by a scale of numbers, nor by adjectives such as substantial, moderate or low. Commentators sometimes used the word punitive but lawyers tended to avoid it because damages were intended to compensate the plaintiff, not punish the defendant, as judges sometimes had to remind a jury champing at the bit with indignation. Exemplary damages were an enhanced sum awarded to show disapproval of the defendant's poor conduct. Damages of £100 could be considered exemplary if £50 was a more usual award in that situation.

Damages assume meaning only when considered in context of a man's annual income, or his capital. Three hundred pounds would be substantial for a successful tradesman, moderate for a successful businessman and low for a man with vast landed estates. Perception of the value of damages also changed over time. At the end of the eighteenth century £500 was moderate. By the early twentieth century it was regarded as substantial.

The average damages in 855 claims won by women between 1791 and 1940 were £365. Ten per cent of awards were for £1,000 or more, scattered throughout the period. The most frequent sum awarded was £100, followed by £50 and then £200. Damages in the local Sheriff's Court were limited to a maximum of £50, however great a woman's loss. Most claims in these courts involved poor couples and £50 was probably an objective measure of what the defendant could afford to pay. When a poor woman was forced to sue a rich man in the Sheriff's Court because she could not afford to bring a claim at the Assizes, better-off men escaped lightly.

Whatever a woman hoped to gain from a breach of promise claim, comparatively few would have expected sufficient damages to provide a permanent, comfortable and independent lifestyle, yet if a woman invested her money sensibly, or disciplined herself to use her capital in a restrained manner then she might avoid having to go out and earn an uncongenial living. A sum of £1,000 invested for a return of three per cent would yield £30 a year at a time when a governess or companion earned between £20 and £40. It meant that a woman living with relatives was not dependant on them. A number of women who won breach of promise cases would have needed to spend their capital to help support themselves and an illegitimate child for several years.

The *Girl's Own Paper* was read by young, unmarried women. In 1891, it published a letter from Mona D. who was 'passing rich on £40 a year'. Mona, a 36-year-old spinster, lodged in one room and, by doing her own cooking and dressmaking, she managed to donate £2 a year to charity and enjoy a modest social life.

Even if damages would not provide a woman with long-term financial security, they were often sufficient to give her the prospect of supporting herself independently, by supplementing any income she could earn. Some women were more enterprising. In 1823, Betsy Hester, daughter of a labouring brewer, planned to use her damages to open a shop. In 1873, Arabella Redhead, a milliner, won £1,750 and considered investing in property to rent out.

A number of awards represented six to twelve months income for a man, or around 20 per cent of his accumulated capital. Many of the larger sums fell within these parameters, indicating that the woman had been compensated for the loss of marriage to a man

(Top) 'The Whim' (1808): A man living life of leisure in pub. Includes the verse 'If ever I marry a wife, / I'll marry a landlord's daughter; / Then I can sit in the bar, / And drink cold brandy & water'. *(Bottom)* 'A Receipt for Courtship' (1805): A suitor hands a note to a young woman *(Library of Congress)*.

'Walking Out': an idealised image of Victorian courtship. *(Author's collection)*

'M.WALKER

R. Taylor

(Top) 'The Suitor Approaches' *(Author's collection)*. *(Bottom Left)* Inch Lane (now Bell Lane), Monmouth: the site of a faked proposal *(Author's collection)*.. *(Bottom Right)* The smallest coin of the realm: from top left, farthings from the reigns of Edward VII, George VI, Victoria, George V *(Author's collection)*.

(*Left*) The Broken Promise': Victorian print *(Author's collection)*. (*Right*) Lewes, whose Assize Court heard many breach of promise claims, including Annie Thomas (1862) and Gladys Knowles (1890) *(Author's collection)*.

Gilbert and Sullivan card, c.1879, showing three operettas, including 'Trial by Jury' at the bottom *(Library of Congress)*.

Damages by Decade awarded by Juries to Female Plaintiffs

Average Damages 1791 - 1920

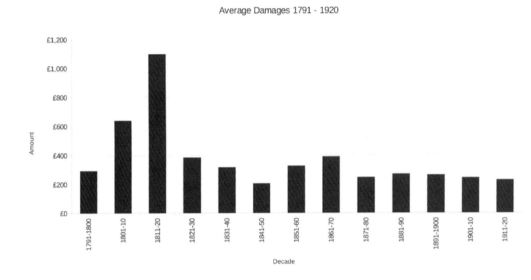

Average Damages at 2012 Values

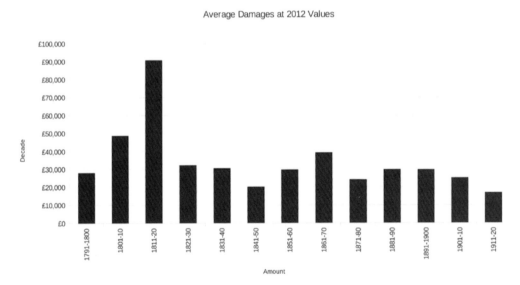

The average damages exclude the extraordinary award of £10,000 to Gladys Knowles in 1890, which was overruled on appeal. They also exclude the awards of £4,000 to Alice Mavro and Charlotte King in 1900, as child maintenance was a key consideration in both cases.

'A Breach of Promise, A Sure Case': print depicting a scene in solicitor's office, c.1895 (*Library of Congress*).

Victorian bride and attendant c.1890 *(Author's collection).*

of substance. Very wealthy men would have suffered little, if any, reduction in lifestyle after paying the damages as their fortune was never at serious risk in a breach of promise claim.

When considered as a percentage of a man's income, some women would have been bitterly disappointed by the damages from rich defendants, as they represented just a few weeks' income or a trivial amount of capital. Lower-class women only obtained substantial damages from a rich man who had behaved in a disgraceful manner and caused them harm. For middle-class ladies with refined feelings, high damages were seen as a birthright, even when the man had behaved in a reasonable way.

Damages for women who worked for a living tended to be low, as these women rarely exhibited any symptoms of a broken heart. Those who prepared for marriage by giving up employment or disposing of a business usually received reasonable compensation but many juries presumed that women who were still working when they were jilted, or had since taken another job to support themselves, needed only nominal damages. In 1868, Martha Booth, a cook, was argued to be better off as a spinster with her £20 annual salary "and the dripping" (a perquisite of the job), than as the wife of a man earning £3 a week. She obtained £10 at the Liverpool Assizes.

Coupled with other similar cases, this strongly suggests that women who worked in manual occupations were considered not to have refined feelings which could be bruised by rejection. In reality, protracted bouts of weeping and lounging in their chamber for several weeks were luxuries only available to middle-class ladies. Those who had to bring in a wage, knew that no matter how upset they felt, if they did not get up and go out to work, they did not get paid.

The cash value of emotional pain was high. In 1870, appeal judges reduced Jane Clarkson's damages from £750 to £500 when Sydney Eisenberg proved that she had suffered no distress after his defection. Extravagant claims about hurt feelings were rarely challenged until the nineteenth century drew to a close. When women were not present in court, juries had to rely on exaggerated descriptions of their grief. When a woman was in court giving evidence it was possible to observe just how much of the bloom in her cheek had faded. In 1899, Florence Dudley replied "I can laugh if I am broken hearted", when asked why she was smiling and whether she was really upset about her broken engagement. She won £200; but within a few years women received little compensation for their heartbreak, unless the defendant had seriously harmed them in some way. Ending an engagement in a needlessly unkind manner was no longer sufficient to warrant any compensation.

Levels of damages awarded reveal notable consistency in the approach of juries to certain issues, indicating that they reflected widely-held social values. Seducing a woman under a promise of marriage was almost always seen as an aggravating feature calling for greater damages. Not many Victorian juries made exceptionally high awards to seduced women, evidence of sexual double standards. Damages for unmarried mothers were probably calculated to enable her and the child to live without parish assistance. Jurors themselves paid the parish rate to support the poor and needy, so it was in their interest to prevent demands upon this. On a more humanitarian basis, most jurors would not want a woman to be forced into the workhouse with her baby if money from the father could prevent it. By the early twentieth century, a change of emphasis can be discerned in two very substantial awards which were intended to enable a rejected woman to give her child an adequate standard of living.

Unwed mothers tended not to receive the highest levels of damages, which may reflect the fact that the majority of illegitimate births were amongst working-class or lower-middle-class women, and their seducers were usually from a similar background. Only 23 per cent of women with an illegitimate child received £100 or less, compared with 48 per cent of those who did not have one. Excluding the distorting effect of awards of £1,000 or more and contemptuous damages, the average amount awarded to a woman who had given birth was £230, compared with £190 for those who were childless. Some of the women who received low damages were already receiving support from the father and this seems to have been taken into account by the jury.

Defendants responded to the particularly generous awards made to unmarried mothers in the early nineteenth century with the short-lived argument that by surrendering her virtue so easily, a disgraced woman proved that she had placed no value on it and should not be generously rewarded for its loss. Judges occasionally found this argument appealing but it gained no favour with juries, possibly because seduction was not confined to working-class women at this time. Jurors may have been thinking of the consequences if their own daughter succumbed to her fiancé.

Towards the end of the nineteenth century, women began to complain of seduction in cases where no child had been conceived. In seduction claims, the average damages were £306, a surprisingly high figure, reflecting the fact that some married men had falsely represented themselves as single. Damages awarded against married seducers rose sharply during the twentieth century, indicating a change in attitude towards obtaining a woman's consent by deception.

An aggravating factor that often led to exemplary damages was unfair or cruel behaviour by a defendant. This took a variety of forms. Juries made substantial awards to mark their disapproval of rich men who broke promises to women of a lower social standing and of poorer men who made or inherited money only to abandon their childhood sweetheart and court a wealthy woman. Nor did they approve of the defendants who sent someone else to break the engagement; pretended to be dead; handed the woman a revolver and told her to shoot herself; broke in and stole letters proving the engagement; organised witnesses to give false evidence; threatened her family; or sent the police to recover presents, alleging that she had stolen them.

Exemplary damages were usually awarded if a man said that his former fiancée had a bad character, but failed to prove it. Even if a woman did have murky aspects to her past it was risky to exploit them. In 1883, Elinor Miller, a widowed hairdresser trading in Bournemouth as Madame Revillon, received a proposal from Henry Joy, a rich property-owner. Before accepting, she arranged for him to be told, in confidence, that she had never been married and her daughter was illegitimate. Initially, Joy declared this made no difference, but when his grown-up children protested about his plans he had second thoughts and ended the engagement, threatening to 'blaze her secret all over town' if she made a claim against him. She did so and ugly rumours began to circulate. Women stopped patronising her salon and her business collapsed. She was awarded £2,500, one of the largest awards ever made. Joy appealed, but his actions were considered 'mean, malignant and injurious' and he was thought particularly spiteful for breaking a confidence.

It is unclear whether juries considered a long engagement as an aggravating factor. Some of these claims also had other aggravating factors and several cases were brought years later to make money when the man married someone else. If a woman had not heard from her 'fiancé' for some time and could not reasonably have believed that he would marry her, then she usually received a very modest award.

A specific category of long engagement involved couples who had lived together for years and possibly had a family. Some cohabited because one of them was not free to wed when the relationship began, while others, for whatever reason, never got round to taking their vows. When a common-law husband walked out, an unmarried woman had no right to maintenance and her only redress was to claim for breach of promise. Juries usually treated these cases as marital breakdown and pragmatically awarded the woman a suitable amount to prevent her becoming a burden on the parish or having to endure much-reduced circumstances.

At the bottom of the damages scale, exemplary awards had a parallel in contemptuous ones. These were very low sums (often a farthing, which was the smallest coin of the realm) awarded when there was a broken promise but when it was considered morally unacceptable for the plaintiff to profit from it. Most successful male claimants received only a small coin and around three per cent of women suffered a similar fate. Contemptuous damages were not restricted to just a few pence. An award of £20 against a wealthy man could reflect a jury's contempt of the way both parties had behaved. Some awards were for out-of-pocket expenses only and provided no compensation for the loss of marriage.

Contemptuous damages were also used to prevent a woman of proven bad character profiting from a broken engagement. The financial value of a lost marriage was at least as great to a promiscuous or a prostitute woman as it was to a virtuous and respectable one and in this respect damages for breach of promise became rooted in a moral judgement of her lifestyle.

Not all women who received contemptuous awards were of bad moral character. Matilda Williams, the daughter of a silk-merchant, received a farthing from Arthur Staples in 1886. Her father had withdrawn his consent to their marriage and Staples decided it was foolhardy to go ahead without it after Matilda's father threatened to kill him if the wedding took place. As public opinion turned decisively against breach of promise in the twentieth century, unless a woman had suffered real harm from a broken engagement, contemptuous damages were used by juries and judges as a blunt but effective instrument to prevent the claim being used for vengeance or to humiliate a defendant.

***

There are hints that high awards were made to compensate middle-class ladies for emotional injury during the late eighteenth century but little firm evidence remains. Average damages began to rise from 1805 when juries may have started to link their award to the value of a life annuity. They peaked at £1,100 between 1816-20, and between 1810-20 four of the ten highest awards of damages by English juries were made, if the twentieth century cases relating to bigamous marriages are excluded. The other six were made in or after 1890 when the value of money had been reduced by inflation.

Damages of £7,000 (currently worth £508,000) were awarded to Mary Alice Orford at Lancaster in 1818, in a claim that lacked any aggravating aspects. Mary was not seduced, her engagement lasted for only two months and the defendant, 22-year-old Thomas Cole, had not behaved in a vicious manner. An unusual feature was age, as Mary was almost 30. Cole argued that she was a mature and calculating woman, who had entrapped him into proposing. The jury chose not to treat this as mitigation and awarded Mary the equivalent of Cole's annual income, whilst the judge refused him permission to appeal, even though the damages were £2,000 more than the previous highest award; an exemplary one arising from the offensive manner in which the defendant had ended the engagement. Precisely what Mr

Robinson had written to Miss Bishop is unknown, as it was too scandalous to be reported by the press.

Four months later, Emma Hardum was awarded £4,000 by a Devonshire jury after she was jilted by a distant cousin. It seems possible that after this verdict senior law officers addressed the use of the annuity method because damages then decreased noticeably. Ann Beathe was also awarded £4,000 in 1820, but her case was exceptional. Not only was Ann the second woman to be jilted by wealthy Samuel Pearson, her distress was such that she spent some weeks in a Manchester lunatic asylum.

In the 1820s average damages plummeted to £385 and by the 1840s they had fallen to £206. Two external factors may be involved. The economy was depressed until the end of the 'hungry forties' and jurors may have felt less generous in harsh economic times, even with other people's money. More significantly, the financial standing of defendants altered as more lower-middle-class men found themselves in court. A claim against a man of moderate means could not be valued as highly as a claim against a rich one.

Cases settled outside court in the 1840s demonstrate that middle-class plaintiffs preferred to negotiate settlements rather than allow their damages to become public knowledge. When Miss Harbottle reputedly received £4,000 from wealthy industrialist John Rylands, in 1845, both parties retained a team of legal specialists to look after their interests. How much a middle-class woman desereved for her broken heart was becoming a matter of conjecture.

During the 1850s, the average level of damages drifted upwards again and peaked at £390 in the following decade, probably reflecting the prosperous economy. High awards became more frequent and created a significant problem for some defendants if juries used damages as a punishment. This led to criticism of breach of promise actions and the competence of juries, particularly in *The Times* which was generally opposed to the claim. In 1865, following two awards of £2,000 made within days of each other, in cases where neither defendant had behaved badly, an editorial pointed out that when deciding damages it was unreasonable to treat all men who jilted a woman as if they had committed a crime.

The change to the ethos of breach of promise claims brought about by the Evidence (Further) Amendment Act 1869 is reflected in average damages which plummeted to £248 in the 1870s, the only decade when almost half of the awards were for £75 or less. Damages decreased because allowing plaintiffs to give evidence stimulated claims by working-class women against men of the same social standing. Even at this lower level, some women were considered to be receiving much more than they deserved. In 1878, a letter in *The Times*, from 'A Barrister' suggested that capricious verdicts would be avoided if female householders sat in the jury box.

In the 1880s, average damages increased to £393, because of the extraordinary award of £10,000 made to Gladys Knowles in 1890. If this one case is excluded, then the more representative average is £271. Similarly, average damages of £351 in the 1890s are skewed by two awards of £4,000 made in quick succession in 1900 to Alice Mavro and Charlotte King against wealthy men who had fathered their children. If these cases are excluded, a plaintiff was more likely to receive £264.

Twenty-one-year-old Gladys Knowles is an enigma. She was reputed to be well-connected but one of her supposed relations wrote to *The Times* denying any relationship. She achieved notoriety in 1890 when she won £10,000 damages, the highest jury award to date for a broken promise of marriage. Public opinion agreed that she had rightly won her case against Leslie Duncan but that, in punishing him for his appalling conduct, the gentlemen of Lewes ignored foolish behaviour by Gladys which led to the conduct she then complained about. It is interesting that, throughout the case, senior judges regarded Gladys solely as a victim.

Leslie Duncan was the proprietor and editor of the *Matrimonial News*, a paper which claimed to have introduced over 40,000 married couples. In 1889, Gladys visited its offices out of curiosity and met 66-year-old Duncan. Within a fortnight the improbable pair were engaged, with Duncan promising a settlement of £1,500 and a further £4,000 on his death. At his invitation, and surprisingly condoned by her mother, Gladys then visited his country home in Sussex for an unchaperoned overnight stay. A few days later she sneaked back for a second visit, expecting to be married as soon as she arrived, but Duncan greeted her with the unwelcome news that the vicar was away. That night, Gladys woke to find her elderly fiancé hovering over her bed. She threatened to leave immediately. When Duncan promised to marry her the next day she decided to stay. Asked in court about why she kept this nocturnal encounter secret for several months, Gladys explained that he had begged her not to ruin his reputation.

The following morning the pair drove to London, where Duncan discovered that he had forgotten to pack the marriage licence and that it was too late to obtain a replacement. As Gladys lived in London, it seems surprising that she went to a hotel with a man who had tried to clamber into her bed the previous night. She said Duncan had promised to take two rooms and when she discovered he had in fact only taken one, she remained fully clothed and went down to the public lounge where she sat until dawn, only returning to the bedroom to avoid curious glances. When day came, Duncan put off the wedding again, dared Gladys to sue him and threatened to tell her titled grandfather about the night in the hotel. Despite his repeated threats and taunts, the engagement continued for a further five months before Gladys and her mother concluded that Duncan had no intention of marrying her.

The judge who summed up was extremely biased against the recently married Duncan, who was travelling in Europe with his wealthy wife. He glossed over the curious features of Gladys's evidence and steered the jury towards punitive damages. The award of £10,000 (currently worth £1.09 million) created an international sensation and was badly received by the press who pointedly asked why Gladys went to a hotel with a man who had already tried to seduce her.

The French magazine, *Gils Blais*, satirised the jury's stupidity, alleging that the fair plaintiff had promised favours to the gullible jurymen. The satire was translated and published in England by *Hawk*, a small circulation paper which was immediately charged with criminal libel for doing so. This was dropped when the editor apologised to Gladys for any inadvertent distress.

Duncan did not pay the damages, so Gladys petitioned for an order declaring him bankrupt. This revealed a problem with bankruptcy law, as there was no way of halting the winding-up of his affairs even though Duncan had appealed against the damages and was expected to obtain a reduction. The bankruptcy proceedings progressed faster than his appeal and Duncan was charged with concealing some of his assets from the Official Receiver as he tried to protect his capital. In 1891, the Appeal Court reduced the damages to £6,500; a sum which recently Gladys had agreed to accept. It can be interpreted as the £5,500 settlement promised by Duncan, plus £1,000 for Gladys's hurt feelings and distress. It still remained an exceptionally large and controversial award.

During the various court hearings, senior judges spoke of the damage a broken engagement caused to a woman's prospects, fearful that such a high profile escapade would severely injure Gladys's chances of finding a husband. They had no need to worry. Two months after the case was finally settled she married Alfred Prager, a London dentist. Duncan disappears from the records and it seems likely that he moved abroad.

Once a method for evaluating damages had been established, judges were happy to follow it. In 1901, a jury awarded Ethel Gardener £3,000 but, after an appeal by Walter Chate, she was given the choice of accepting £1,500 or facing a new trial. The judges emphasised that the jurors had been swayed by their emotions and disregarded the law.

During the Edwardian era, the value of breach of promise claims continued to plummet. This may be linked to the fact that men who had grown to adulthood in a society which increasingly saw breach of promise as a shabby and discreditable action were now being called for jury service. In the decade to 1920, the average award was only £230. A woman's damages became more clearly related to her actual financial losses and the principles of contract law were reasserted. It was impossible for a woman to reap a windfall harvest without extenuating circumstances.

After 1920, averages lack meaning. Damages had evolved into specific responses to individual cases and no longer considered hurt feelings or loss of marriage as they sorted out questions of bigamy and property disputes. The highest individual award in a breach of promise case was made in 1951 with a punitive award of £20,000, though after an appeal and a second trial this was reduced to £11,000; still a substantial sum though not as generous as the £7,000 to Mary Alice Orford in 1818.

Having lost her man, winning a claim against him did not guarantee that a woman would get her money either. This depended on whether the man could afford to pay; an issue many jurors overlooked. Up to ten per cent of cases involved a request to appeal, even if permission to challenge the decision was not forthcoming. Only a small number of those told to pay high damages tried to appeal, which suggests that however annoyed the men were about the outcome they could afford the award. The majority of appeals were from defendants told to pay a few hundred pounds. There were legal costs involved in an appeal, and most were unsuccessful, so those who took this path must have had serious concerns about their ability to raise the funds. Relatively few outcomes of appeals were reported by the press, which strongly implies that they were usually resolved by private negotiation rather than a judge. There were probably informal negotiations between the parties where an appeal was not made if the man genuinely could not pay.

Suing a working-class man rarely led to financial satisfaction as they struggled to find small sums and usually had to pay by instalments. After 1880, judges regularly advised jurors to be restrained in awards against working men if they wanted the woman to receive anything. By 1921, instalments of breach of promise damages were notorious as an obligation that men ignored, alongside maintenance for a former wife, forcing women to apply to the courts for a payment order. Paying by instalments could take years and prevented working-class plaintiffs and defendants from putting a broken engagement behind them, though for the plaintiff a few shillings a week was probably a more accurate reflection of any advantage marriage would have brought than receiving her money as a lump sum.

If a man was determined not to pay, then it was relatively simple to move to another part of the country, informally adopt a different name and become untraceable. Emigration offered another escape route. Dr Pickburn sailed for Sydney the day before Louisa Woodley's claim against him was heard, sending his father to court to explain his absence. The case went ahead and Louisa was awarded £650, but it seems unlikely that she received it. Another group of women who may have only won a moral victory were those who sued foreign men. Some plaintiffs received generous compensation in unacknowledged or undefended cases, though it is improbable that a woman would succeed in enforcing a breach of promise judgement from an English court in a foreign country.

Around 10 per cent of cases scheduled for a court hearing were resolved without the input of a jury. Terms were not always disclosed, but where they were plaintiffs tended to receive good outcomes, often exceeding the average damages then being awarded by juries, with defendants probably motivated to be generous by potential savings in the legal bills. Another factor was brinkmanship and hard negotiation. Some defendants were prepared to pay handsomely to ensure that sentimental or compromising letters were not read out in public. A number of cases were settled overnight or during a lunch-break when part of the case had been aired and barristers for both sides could assess the preliminary reaction of the jury.

Some plaintiffs reluctantly accepted a low sum after their case made a bad impression. Ann Hunt was jilted in 1804 when her fiancé dispatched his errand boy to church to stop the banns being called. Unfortunately, her principal witness gave his evidence so ineptly that he made the claim sound ridiculous to everyone in court. Unable to retrieve the situation, silver-tongued barrister William Garrow decided it was better to settle for £10 and Ann's costs rather than risk the jury finding in the defendant's favour.

Settled cases were not necessarily combative, especially when the couple were of unequal social standing. One common theme is a man from a wealthy family who had been separated by parental or social pressures from a woman he was genuinely attached to. While an undergraduate at Cambridge, Joseph Lyle, heir to a substantial estate in Helston, Cornwall fell in love with Emily Coulden, the daughter of a local craftsman. When Lyle graduated his father appears to have refused him permission to marry her. Emily claimed for breach of promise, and Lyle probably infuriated his family when he refused to say a word against her, acknowledged that the end of their engagement was his fault alone and agreed to pay £1,000, which would have given her financial security for life. Ironically, within ten years, Lyle mortgaged his life-interest in the estate and emigrated to New Zealand to avoid bankruptcy.

Peers' sons feature in several high value settlements to actresses. May Finney, known professionally as Miss Fortescue, sued Lord Garmoyle, heir to Earl Cairns, in 1884. The settlement of £10,000 was concluded in court, so that her character could be vindicated by his public confirmation that 'throughout the whole engagement, from its inception to its termination, there was nothing in the bearing or conduct of Miss Finney that was in any degree unbecoming a high-minded English gentlewoman'. The largest known settlement for a breach of promise claim was made in 1913, by the Marquis of Northampton to Daisy Mons, after family pressures had intervened to end their engagement. She received £50,000, (currently worth £4.9 million), almost five times more than an English jury ever awarded in any other breach of promise claim.

Excluding cases of bigamy or cohabitation, the highest levels of compensation for a broken engagement were more easily obtained by negotiation than awarded by a jury. As the results of some settled cases remain secret and other claims were never listed for a court hearing, it seems likely that negotiation provided the best outcome when a defendant was sincere about paying realistic but affordable damages. This was more apparent to gentleman's daughters than to poorer women who, by refusing to negotiate, frequently condemned themselves to the frustration of not receiving what they were awarded by a jury. Despite this, they established their unsullied character, an advantage lost by women whose public claim was unsuccessful.

Chapter 7

The Court of Public Opinion
Women who failed with Breach of Promise Claims

*If juries in breach of promise cases are to give verdicts
according to law and common sense, it is evident that
we are on the verge of a revolution.*
(Editorial, *The Guardian*, 12 August 1875)

The triumph of female plaintiffs in breach of promise cases was so
well publicised in the nineteenth century press that it is surprising
to discover just how many claims ended in failure. Ten per cent
of women taking a claim before a jury were unsuccessful. Others
won their cases but received damages that were contemptuous or
so low that they caused intense disappointment.

In 1853, Harriet Goodman had Charles Young arrested for
criminal perjury after his evidence about her lewd conduct
resulted in her being awarded just £50 damages from Edward
Pegg. At a preliminary hearing to discover whether there was a
case for Young to answer, the judge decided there was no reason
to prosecute him and told Harriet to pursue a private remedy if
she felt his evidence was untruthful.

The success rate for women varied. Before 1805 it was around
80 per cent, though between 1816 and 1850 more than 95 per cent
of women won their cases. After 1870, the rate dropped back to
around 80 per cent. In the years before the Great War it rose to
90 per cent, which can probably be explained by falling levels of
damages reducing the incentive to bring weak claims.

Several factors explain why not all women plaintiffs were
successful. One was the jury system. It is a feature of jury trials
that different groups of people can reach varying conclusions
based on exactly the same information. For no obvious reason,
a woman might lose an argument that countless others regularly

won. It was also rare for a jury to accept a man's uncorroborated word that a woman had released him from their engagement. Now barely discernible factors, such as the shifty body-language of the plaintiff or one of her witnesses, may be the reason why jurors very occasionally preferred the man's version of events.

For a few women, the jury's negative conclusion seems capricious in the extreme. In 1834, a London jury awarded Miss Want a shilling when her intended went off with her money and the household goods she had bought in anticipation of their marriage and wed another woman. The verdict was greeted with astonishment by everyone in court.

At least two juries seem not have taken their task as seriously as they should have and prioritised getting home for the evening above a thorough assessment of the evidence. Both unexpectedly found for the defendant as the court's working day ended, which meant that they did not have to spend more time agreeing the level of damages. Twelve good men from Huddersfield were on the point of being locked in for the night in 1863, when they suddenly discovered that they all believed the defendant's story. In London in 1908, even the judge expressed surprise when Violet Carr lost after just ten minutes deliberation by the jurymen. He remarked to her shocked lawyer that the jury could not be wrong, but sent out a stern instruction to Herbert Watermeyer to be moderate in his bill for costs.

Breach of promise was often out of step with influential public opinion and, from the 1850s until the naughty nineties, newspapers criticised jurors for verdicts that took no account of the law or common sense. Some juries appear to have bent over backwards to help a woman to obtain a bit of money for herself, condoning some very impudent claims supported by negligible evidence of a proposal.

A woman's advantage ended in 1869 when the Evidence (Further) Amendment Act stipulated that a proposal must be corroborated by evidence other than the word of a plaintiff and that such evidence should be of a good standard. In the next decade, as judges worked out what was a good standard of corroborating evidence, their decisions gradually tipped the balance against working-class women if men of means denied a proposal. Detriment to poor but honest women was probably never intended by legislators, but senior judges who interpreted the evidence requirements sometimes seem too ready to sanction the conduct of men who exploited women and turned their backs on the consequences.

Corroboration could take many forms such as a letter, a ring or even speaking about the engagement in front of a third party. An astute man could sweet-talk a woman in private, avoid any mention of marriage in public, write no letters and ensure that his gifts did not include anything that might be interpreted as an engagement ring. Sexual intimacy was usually involved when a woman sued a man of a much higher social standing than her own and judges found it difficult to believe that a wealthy and successful man might make an offer of marriage to entice a poor woman into his bed.

In 1876, a young actress, Artie Colebrook, was unable to prove a promise by Michael Ralli, a prosperous Liverpool cotton broker. The couple had lived together for five years and she gave up theatrical work at his request. She claimed that her decision to move in with him sprang from a promise which he repeated several times over the years, but found excuse after excuse not to fulfil. In his defence, Ralli produced letters written on his behalf, enclosing Artie's monthly allowance after he tricked her into leaving the house they had shared. As she had not disputed the contents of the letters, he argued they proved that Artie agreed that she had lived as his mistress. Assertions in letters written after Ralli ended the relationship do not prove that he had not strung her along for years with verbal promises of marriage but Artie's witness was not believed by the jury and she lost her claim.

That same year, a clandestine relationship developed between a young German servant, Catherine Bessila, and the son of a Liverpool merchant, David Sterne, who was at least ten years her senior. When Catherine became pregnant he abandoned her. Catherine was awarded £100 by the jury hearing her case but, rather than pay her anything, Sterne challenged the verdict, claiming that her evidence did not meet the legal standard. Catherine's sister had a conversation with Sterne before the baby was born and he said that he would do whatever was necessary to avoid a scandal. He said this did not refer to marriage but to paying for her to return to Germany with the baby. After the birth Catherine's sister heard her reproaching Sterne, saying that he kept promising to marry her but never did so. He made no reply to her accusation.

Sterne's argument was upheld, two judges agreeing that this evidence was not sufficient corroboration. The case then went to a further appeal where three senior judges reluctantly found in Catherine's favour, deciding that supporting evidence did not have to be strong but must be unambiguous. They also added that disallowing Catherine's claim would affect many other plaintiffs whose supporting evidence was often no stronger than that given by Catherine's sister.

As the century progressed, the evidence standard became ever-tighter and it became impossible for a woman to argue that the man's conduct demonstrated his intention to marry her. Several judges were remarkably quick to decide that a man's behaviour towards a woman was more consistent with establishing her as his mistress than preparing to make her his wife. Even posing as a married couple was not sufficient to prove any promise, as a gentleman might pretend to be married to spare a woman embarrassment, as Charles Levy had done when he told Elizabeth Ross to introduce him as her husband when her mother and sister came to visit.

In a handful of cases the law appeared to condone prosperous men seducing poor women with promises they never intended to keep. Judges upheld the letter of the law, even when the man had deliberately stolen the woman's evidence. In 1900, Charles Mobberley met and then seduced Rosa Owen whilst they were both working in India. As she lay ill in bed he cynically went into her room and removed some of his letters, depriving her of any proof of his proposal. He then ignored her solicitor's request to return them. The enhanced evidence requirements intended to protect men from false claims had handed the worldly-wise a way to exploit women with apparent impunity.

By the 1890s, working-class men also defended claims by arguing that a woman had chosen to become their mistress with no expectation of marriage. Perhaps no story says more about the seedy underbelly of late-Victorian and Edwardian life than the experiences of 19-year-old Edith Faulkner, a poor but respectable young teacher who went to London to try to find work. On her journey to the capital, naïve Edith fell into the clutches of William Turnpenny, a predatory older man who introduced himself with a false name and, as Edith discovered later, used around 20 different aliases to disguise his nefarious activities. Turnpenny seduced her with promises of marriage, which quickly turned to dust when she discovered he was a married man. He beat her, laced her food with noxious drugs to induce a miscarriage, accused her of drunkenness and tried to lure her into prostitution.

He defended Edith's claim for breach of promise, arguing that a woman who expected marriage would leave a man's house as soon as she learned that he had a wife. Edith had no choice but to remain when she discovered the deception because she had nowhere else to live and no money to support herself. The jury found in Turnpenny's favour on the breach of promise claim, but ordered him to pay her £150 as damages for assault and administering noxious drugs.

***

Breach of promise was not an ideal way of resolving the consequences of failed sexual relationships and when the couple consisted of a poor woman and a man from the establishment it was difficult for the woman to obtain a fair hearing. This was vividly demonstrated when 25-year-old Annie Thomas lost her claim against Major General Arthur Shirley in 1862, though she won in the court of public opinion. Incensed by the way Shirley and the legal system had treated her, a few readers of *The Times* subscribed to a fund to pay her legal costs.

Annie had advertised incognito for a situation as a housekeeper to a widower or single man, which Shirley portrayed as a scheme to entrap. If she was baiting such a trap, then a man of intelligence ought to have spotted this and a man of honour would have avoided answering. There was no shortage of people seeking work in 1861 so Annie was not the only available candidate for employment.

Shirley was separated from his wife but told Annie he was

a widower. Twice her age, he had immoral intentions from the outset. Within days she was living in his home and known as Mrs Shirley, a situation which lasted until she became pregnant. Annie had no witnesses to confirm her contention that Shirley had offered her marriage. He denied her allegation, described her as a blackmailer and claimed to be resisting her lies as a matter of honour. Public statements that he would provide for the child and would not accept costs from her if she lost the case created the impression that he was both a man of honour and an innocent victim of a designing woman.

In 1862, the law did not yet require corroboration of a proposal and when a woman had no witnesses the judge usually told the jury to decide whether or not they thought the woman had relied on a promise. When seduction was involved, juries usually took the view that the woman would have surrendered under a promise of marriage. In Annie's case the judge summed up in a very biased manner, branding her an extortioner and virtually instructing the jury to find for Shirley. Annie appealed for a new trial because of this bias. The hearing was inexplicably hostile, especially when her barrister revealed that since the trial she had obtained corroboration that Shirley had promised marriage. The court refused to allow a retrial. It was seen at the time as the establishment closing ranks to protect its own and begs the question of where the decision to find in Shirley's favour originated, as he had connections to the aristocracy as well as the army.

Public opinion had no doubt that Shirley was a heartless and immoral seducer. In court, Annie's advertisement was used as evidence of ill intent on her part but there is no other evidence that she was of bad character and previous employers described her as a respectable young woman. It was not unusual for woman to receive a proposal after accepting a position as housekeeper and possibly the worst that can be said about Annie was that she was naïve in the way she tried to find employment with a man who might be looking for a wife.

A generation later, establishment attitudes had not changed. In 1891, a German governess, Valerie Weidermann, finally ran out of options in her three-year court battle against Robert Walpole, heir to the Earldom of Orford. Walpole acknowledged a brief sexual relationship with Valerie in Turkey but argued that he had only ever intended her to be his mistress. Much about their relationship is ambiguous and it is impossible to be certain whether Valerie was a victim or a villainess, though there was some public sympathy for her.

The case had two hearings and two appeals. Valerie was not allowed to bring evidence she believed would prove an engagement. Instead, she was forced to rely on letters she had written to Walpole, which he had ignored. The second jury to hear the case awarded Valerie £300 for breach of promise and libel. This related to a ring of Walpole's in Valerie's possession. She said that he had given it to her when they parted. Walpole alleged that she had stolen it from him. The Appeal Court overruled the breach of promise verdict and ordered her to pay Walpole's legal costs. In the circumstances this was vindictive as the wealthy Walpole had failed to overturn the libel decision against him. In direct contrast to Michael Ralli's case, letters written by Valerie asserting a fact Walpole had not disputed, were not accepted as evidence to prove Valerie's case. Winning a claim for breach of promise was virtually impossible for a working-class woman when a man with money and connections was determined to defeat it.

Discarded mistresses with no means of their own faced a precarious future as an unmarried partner had no claim for financial support at the end of the relationship, irrespective of why it had ended, how long it had lasted and her contribution to the family home and life. As the law offered no other redress, some women brought a claim hoping that a jury would find in their favour, or that a man could be shamed into doing the decent thing and provide for them. Usually, if a man of means wanted to end a relationship he would anticipate any potential unpleasantness or publicity by arranging to pay the woman a regular allowance to enable her to live modestly but respectably and provide for any children the couple had. These informal maintenance arrangements often had strings attached, preventing the woman from bringing a claim for breach of promise or contacting her former lover except via his solicitor.

When a man refused to provide for his ex-mistress and family all a woman could do was obtain a maintenance order for the children at the normal parish rate. In trying to force Thomas Hunt to allow her reasonable maintenance for their children, Stockton dressmaker, Harriet Spiers brought a landmark case in 1907, which established the legal position of a woman who received a promise from a married man to make her his wife when he became free to do so. Thomas Hunt had promised to marry her when his wife died, but refused to keep his word when he became free. When Harriet appealed against the decision by a lower court, senior judges decided as a matter of public policy that a woman could not receive damages for a promise made to her by a man if she knew that he was married when he made it.

The facts of Harriet's situation were sad. Hunt, a wealthy man, was turned 70 when their relationship commenced in 1899 and Harriet around 30. His wife was some years older, in poor health and not expected to survive for much longer. Hunt's promise of marriage when he became a widower induced Harriet to become his mistress and their relationship produced four children. After five years Hunt's interest in her waned. He accused her of infidelity, denied paternity of her youngest child and withdrew financial support from the family, forcing Harriet to take him to court. He produced no evidence that he was not the father of the child and the court ordered him to maintain all four children.

Despite her bad health Mrs Hunt lived until 1907. Harriet then asked Hunt to honour his promise and marry her, but he refused. There was by now no residual affection on either side. Harriet was hoping to obtain better support from him for their children, either by an increased allowance for them or with her damages for breach of promise. Hunt chose to fight her claim, arguing that it was an affront to public morality for a married man to promise to wed another woman, as such a promise was likely to weaken the marriage bond and lead to immoral conduct.

Harriet was cast as the author of her own misfortunes for relying on a promise that a moral woman would have known was wrong and allowing herself to be seduced by a married man. Hunt suffered scant condemnation for making a promise he too must have known was wrong, in order to effect the seduction. This attitude was a symptom of a culture that allowed men much more latitude than women in matters of sexual conduct. The only apparent criticism of Hunt was a comment by one of the judges that it was poor conduct if a man of his financial standing refused to make better provision for his children.

Until this case was decided, women who unwittingly accepted proposals from married men were awarded damages for breach of promise if they could prove the offer of marriage. The decision against Harriet Spiers had the potential to rob duped women of any redress if the mere fact of a marriage vow protected the man. Courts refused to sanction men citing marriage as a defence in any situation where he had deceived the woman.

In 1919, Adele Reynaud, a Frenchwoman who came to England to perfect her language skills was awarded £650 from London theatre producer John Martin. They had lived together for some years after he suggested marriage and she had a child by him, believing that he was divorced. In 1936, Amme Beyers received £8,000 after discovering that Thomas Green, who had portrayed himself as a bachelor, had a wife. When rumours of this had reached her before their wedding, Amme had asked Green if he was free to marry her and he had confirmed that he was.

Success in claims against married men required a woman's conduct to be above reproach and this could involve showing an unrealistic amount of diligence. Even when a woman was successful, the damages could reflect a value judgement about her conduct. In an age when poor women did not have access to good education or well-paid employment, it was harsh to pretend that they should have known when to make enquiries about a man and how to make them, or that they could afford to pay someone to carry out the task. In 1915, Lilian Cooper left tennis player Horace Chapman when she discovered their recent marriage was bigamous, but she received only a farthing because she was deemed reckless in going through a marriage ceremony without proof that he was divorced. Unusually, the judge ordered Chapman to pay her legal costs, suggesting that he disagreed with the jury's contemptuous award of damages.

If a man with some money at his disposal was determined to fight a claim, then poor women faced having their reputation attacked. They were particularly susceptible to allegations of old immoralities, as bad character discovered after a proposal gave a man grounds to end his engagement. Evidence about a woman's past conduct was not regularly put before a jury, but it appears that the tactic was used as a lever by the man's legal representatives to negotiate an out-of-court settlement.

Men sometimes resorted to discrediting the woman, sparing little effort to secure their evidence and possibly blackening her and character unjustifiably. Some men left no stone unturned and managed to discover their escape-route at the eleventh hour. Seduced and then abandoned by a married man who pretended to be single, Millicent Milner withdrew her case when the defence attempted to introduce some information about her described as medical. Her barrister said that she would abandon her claim rather than have personal details discussed in court.

***

Some women lost their claim for breach of promise because they faced a determined, possibly unscrupulous man. Other men had every reason to defend a claim vigorously because it was fraudulent. The most remarkable was the fabric of lies woven by Mary Elizabeth Smith in 1846. Her claim against Earl Ferrers saw the public gallery crammed at an early hour of the first day. On the third morning, the rush to find a space when the door opened 'resembled the crush at the Opera House'. The case generated souvenir supplements and pamphlets in addition to blow-by-blow newspaper coverage.

Mary was the 21-year-old daughter of a Warwickshire gentleman. In 1839, Earl Ferrers, then a teenager, boarded in the neighbourhood with his tutor; a standard stage in the education of a young nobleman. Mary alleged that she had become acquainted with Ferrers at this time, and that when a mutual affection developed between them he had promised to marry her. Ferrers at this point was under 21, so any promise would have been invalid. Mary's parents were clearly worried about something because when they discovered the alleged engagement they sent her to London and then to France for several months, until Ferrers had moved abroad to begin the next part of his education.

Mary returned to Warwickshire and in 1842 she claimed to

have received a letter from Ferrers reaffirming his promise. Over the next few months the couple apparently corresponded frequently and Ferrers told her to buy various articles as presents for herself and that he would pay the bills. Her father received letters from Ferrers asking him to settle the accounts and to make arrangements for the wedding, which he did. Throughout the months when Mary wrote to Ferrers, relatives, servants and friends posted the letters for her. When reports of Earl Ferrers's engagement and later his marriage to Lady Augusta Chichester appeared in the newspapers in the early summer of 1844 Mary immediately issued a claim for breach of promise.

Shocked to receive the claim, Earl Ferrers refuted her allegations completely. He denied the correspondence between them or having made any promise of marriage when he lived with his tutor. He recollected seeing Mary at church but could not remember whether they had spoken or not. If they had, then their conversation left no trace in his memory.

Three days of evidence centred on the letters to Mary and her father. Ferrers claimed they were forged. Witnesses were produced by both parties to try to identify or disprove his handwriting. Some said the writing bore a similarity to Mary's, others thought it was definitely his. Mary's young sister, 13-year-old Ann Smith, told the court that Ferrers had visited their house, unwisely mentioning a specific date.

On the third day of the hearing Mary's claims began to unravel. Ferrers could not have made the alleged visit to her home on the date Ann Smith recalled, because he had been with his sister and brother-in-law, 60 miles away. Details about Ferrers in some of the letters were also wrong. His brother gave evidence and denied writing any letters telling Mary that her wedding needed to be postponed because Ferrers was in a serious fever or enclosing his ring for her.

Early in the trial, when Mary's mother gave evidence, Ferrers's barrister asked her to confirm whether four documents he produced were in Mary's writing. She did so. During the third afternoon he revealed that Earl Ferrers had received a number of letters from an anonymous lady and these were four surviving letters which he had forgotten to burn. The style and phrasing was similar to that of the letters Ferrers denied writing. The next morning, with Mary unable to explain these letters, her legal team withdrew their services and her case collapsed.

The story gripped the country and interest continued for some time. Mary was widely condemned by public opinion and may have been lucky not to face criminal charges. Six months later she issued a pamphlet, explaining that she had been wronged and reiterating the engagement to Ferrers. Her pamphlet was not well-received and the *Britannia Newspaper* branded her a liar. Mary then sued for libel. The case was decided in her favour on a technicality, but she received only a farthing in damages and was left to settle her own costs.

Why Mary carried a fantasy about Ferrers to this extent has never been satisfactorily explained. Nor is the role of her family clear. Although the family declared that they believed Mary and Ferrers were engaged, Mr Smith appears unduly lax in settling large bills for clothes and trinkets and organising his daughter's wedding without even meeting the prospective bridegroom or arranging practicalities such as her marriage settlement. Ann Smith's artless recollection of the Earl's visits was untruthful, but coming from a young girl it was likely to add credence to the case. Had a few anonymous letters not escaped the flames, the apparent weight of evidence on Mary's side may easily have convinced the jury to award her substantial damages.

Mary was not alone in bringing a false claim, but it was unusual for a middle-class woman to do so. Fraudulent claims tended to come from poor women for whom the temptation of a few pounds proved too great to resist. A 26-year-old barmaid, Ella Wells, was more typical in trying to obtain money from a man who owed her nothing. In 1891, she unexpectedly claimed damages for an engagement broken two years earlier by a bar manager she had occasionally walked out with. Shortly before her case came to court she wrote to tell a London policeman that she would be unable to contact him for a few weeks and that her sister would explain why. Confronted by this letter in the witness box, Ella could not explain why she sent love and kisses and assured him that everything would be all right for them in a few weeks' time. The London jury found for the relieved publican.

Despite public perception, breach of promise fraud was not limited to women. Two months before Ella Wells was exposed, Gladys Evelyn was wrongly labelled an extortioner when William Hurlbert lied on oath to deny that he had written a number of compromising letters to her. He claimed the author was a man named Charles Murray, who had remarkably similar handwriting. The jury found for Hurlbert but the case became subject to a criminal investigation because it was obvious that either the plaintiff or defendant had committed perjury. Gertrude was able to provide further evidence confirming her claims, but before Hurlbert could be questioned he hastily returned to America and then travelled on to Mexico to thwart arrest.

**

There were several defences available to justify breaking a promise to marry and a few unlucky women lost their claim because the man had a valid defence. Very occasionally, a man proved to the court that he was unsuited for the married state. In 1861, the children of retired cleric John Pridham, an 80-year-old suffering from dementia, defeated a claim from 50-year-old Susannah Clampitt, a comely draper from Exeter. In what was probably a no-cure-no-pay action, members of the Clampitt family clubbed together to guarantee the £20 loan, which enabled her to sue Pridham for £1,000 after receiving his unexpected proposal.

Susannah contended that Pridham was a healthy man of sound mind and fully aware of the implications of his offer. His children demonstrated that his fragile mental condition was well-known locally and argued that even if Susannah had not enticed him into making the offer, she was trying to take advantage of words the old man no longer understood the meaning of. He had already spent a period in an asylum, had no memory from one day to the next and not infrequently proposed marriage to acquaintances and sometimes to imaginary women. After a letter to an imaginary woman called Margaret was read out in court, Susannah's barrister, somewhat embarrassed to be representing her, withdrew the claim. The judge commented that the Pridham family had acted properly in resisting the demands made of their father.

Bad conduct by a woman after their engagement also entitled a man to change his mind about marriage. In 1869, a tailor named Abrahams ended his engagement to Julia Barnett when she told him that a guard on the Metropolitan Railway had taken liberties with her in a railway carriage. She refused to identify him or report what had happened, probably hoping to forget about her ordeal. When she subsequently gave birth to a son, she named her former fiancé as the father and her relatives said that he had visited mother and child and acknowledged the child as his. Abrahams explained that he had been tricked into visiting the house under false pretences and her family then tried to coerce him to agree to marry her. With discrepancies in the evidence of Julia's witnesses, the court believed his story and accepted that her involuntary conduct with the railway guard absolved him from his promise of marriage.

Sometimes the courts agreed with a man's view that his offer of marriage had been conditional and the conditions had not been fulfilled. Solicitor's widow Sophia Loveday asked William Moore to settle £2,000 on her. He agreed to make a settlement but refused to withdraw capital from his coffee house to fund this. He offered £1,000, arguing that £2,000 would result in the business being damaged and his income reduced, affecting the standard of living he could offer his future wife. After four attempts to negotiate terms failed he ended the discussions and decided not to marry her, even though she then offered to marry him without any settlement. The hearing decided that his promise was conditional on the couple agreeing a marriage settlement and dismissed her claim. Sophia appealed for that verdict to be set aside on the grounds that the judge had misdirected the jury. Other judges confirmed that she could not try to impose conditions she had no right to insist on and then sue for breach of promise when they were not agreed to.

The court criticised the foolish advice Sophia had received from friends telling her to hold out for £2,000. She lost her own wealth when her father failed to protect her interests with a marriage settlement and her husband squandered the money, leaving her a penniless widow reliant on the goodwill of friends for a home. She had been fortunate to receive a proposal from someone who could have provided her with a settled home, a comfortable lifestyle and some security if she was widowed for a second time.

Some cases were very unusual and cannot be categorised. Annie Mendoza served a writ for breach of promise before the wedding day. Her hasty action allowed Israel Ruben to prove that he had never refused to marry her and to escape from the engagement with impunity.

In 1893, no-one appeared to query the circumstances in which Jenny Mighel received a proposal from the Sultan of Johore in Malaysia. Perhaps wisely, the court declined to hear any details, stating that it had no jurisdiction over a foreign monarch. In 1964, *The Guardian* reported that the Sultan was actually a Mr Albert Baker, who had played fast and loose with Jenny's affections.

A few women who were initially successful saw the verdict overturned on appeal. Lack of corroborating evidence was one factor. Another was new evidence coming to light indicating that the woman might have lied. In 1877, 32-year-old Sarah Deane from Leicester was deprived of £150 from an elderly vicar, Thomas Oldacres. After losing the case he employed a private detective to look into her background and discovered that she had served a prison sentence for theft and compromised two other claims for breach of promise. This did not prove that Oldacres had not broken a promise, but it meant that if Sarah wanted damages she would have to pay her legal costs in another hearing where this new evidence would be considered. Lawyers were unlikely to offer a no-cure-no-pay arrangement in these circumstances.

Some claimants were proved to be fraudulent. In June 1914, 57-year-old Catherine Francis was jailed for six months for aggravated perjury, after stating she was a widow and lying about her age to divert attention from an incriminating marriage certificate. Although she was not living with her husband, he was paying her a regular allowance so this was not the innocent mistake of a long-deserted woman. Doris Burton, an actress known as Doritza Dulibert, won £750 from Hatton Garden diamond merchant George Dresden in 1916, but lost it a few months later when he obtained proof that her husband was still living. In 1930, Doris, by then known as Gee, was jailed for blackmailing a vicar.

***

In addition to those whose claims were not upheld, another group of women, although successful, were awarded trivial or contemptuous damages and sometimes deprived of their costs from the defendant. They usually received a farthing, or occasionally a shilling. After the Great War, damages were increasingly restricted to actual expense incurred and no award was made to compensate for the loss of marriage. Often the women receiving contemptuous awards were presented as grasping and nasty in newspaper reports. This could have been influenced by the outcome of the case but it also adds credence to other evidence that a pleasing personality and appearance was likely to find favour with jurymen.

Contemptuous damages signalled that the jury disapproved of the claim, thought the woman had suffered no loss as a result of the broken promise or refused to allow her to enrich herself unfairly. Juries did not like women who were clearly trying to take advantage of a man who did not know what he was doing. In 1838, when Lancashire milliner Mary Ann Wilde sued John Atherton for £200 she received a farthing. There was doubt about whether Atherton was sober when he proposed after a five-day courtship and his counsel asked what Mary Ann lost by not being married to a chronic alcoholic. The jury decided that she had no wish to be his wife and that she was trying to use words uttered when she knew he was drunk to relieve him of a portion of his capital.

Annie Jacobs received a farthing from a Leeds glass manufacturer after the muddled content of one of her letters led him to believe that she had terminated their brief engagement. The jury decided that Samuel Woolf was mistaken in the belief that he was free to pay his addresses to someone else, but refused to let Annie profit from the innocent mistake. All her requests and correspondence with him during their engagement were tinged with mercenary motives.

A very unusual case was heard in 1905 when Michael McCarthy sued Thomas Kennedy on behalf of a jilted girl known only as Miss L. Legal action could be taken on another person's behalf as a matter of charity, to ensure access to justice for someone who could not afford to bring their own claim. If the case was successful the benefactor could expect to be reimbursed the costs of his generosity by the defendant. Although Kennedy was proved to have jilted Miss L, the court realised that MacCarthy's motives were not charitable and that he was trying to ruin Kennedy with damages and costs. He won a farthing for Miss L from the jury and the judge refused to award him the legal fees.

From 1920 contemptuous awards became more frequent. In 1921, Surrey widow Winifred Coates received a farthing when she sued William Cromwell. The pair had known each other for many years as family friends and Cromwell had told her at one point that he would have married her if she had been free. She alleged that he proposed to her ten days after her husband died, a conversation he denied, though a maid who had been listening outside the room confirmed Winifred's story. The judge described the case as oppressive and one that should never have been brought, as decent people would be shocked by a married woman talking about being another man's wife, or a widow accepting a proposal ten days after her husband died in the service of his country. Depriving her of costs warned other women not to bring claims that scandalised right-thinking people.

With four out of five women succeeding in their claim for more than nominal damages, breach of promise was a case that a woman was always more likely to win than lose. A few victories were pyrrhic, resulting in very low damages and leaving the woman out-of-pocket. Some of those who lost were deservedly exposed as devious schemers, or grasping women on the make in situations that offended the values of the time. Others were unable to meet legal requirements for evidence of a promise. Occasionally a decision reflected the unpredictability of the jury system. A small number of cases from the later Victorian and Edwardian period appear to sanction the exploitation of poor women by unscrupulous men and raise one ugly question: why?

Chapter 8

Debt, Despair, Divorce and Death
The Dark Side of Breach of Promise

Dear Sir, Please give me a call at your earliest convenience,
otherwise an action of a serious nature will be
commenced against you.
(Letter from a blackmailer, *The Times*, 1 June 1889)

Until the Great War, the British public savoured a juicy breach of promise case, at least in private. For more than a century, many newspapers drip-fed a steady diet of titillation, publishing salacious hints of illicit sexual encounters and embarrassing letters from love-lorn swains which provided a cruel laugh at the misfortunes of others.

The trial of Bardell and Pickwick remained popular for many years, with Dickens occasionally giving public readings of the court scene. In the early twentieth century, the comedy was given a boost by Vesta Victoria's popular music hall character, a naïve, marriage hungry spinster, who was left 'waiting at the church' when Obadiah Binks sent his note of insincere apology which read,

> *Can't get away to marry you today.*
> *My wife won't let me.*

For those with no personal experience, breach of promise signified comedy or melodrama, peopled with distressed, beautiful young heroines, villainous cads who could afford the damages and deserved to be brought down a peg or two, sexual shenanigans to be tutted over and, occasionally, older women caricatured as pantomime dames. This picture was widely peddled by a press which trivialised the pain of broken engagements in order to provide their readerships with the level of scandal they craved.

A darker, more disturbing reality lurked within those same newspapers. For a woman, a breach of promise claim might be her only redress for a crime committed against her. In 1863, Alfred Cleveland was told by a judge that he had no case to answer when Margaret Sparrow complained that he had obtained £100 by false pretences to prepare for their marriage. His Lordship said that Margaret could try to recover her lost savings with a claim for breach of promise. In 1900, Florence Jones was drugged and raped by a chemist. A solicitor and her employer advised her to sue for breach of promise. Only when Natalio Polombi rebuffed the claim was the attack reported to the police, who charged him with attempted poisoning. He received 15 months' hard labour for an offence that did not fully reflect the gravity of the ordeal he had inflicted upon his victim.

Trials in the criminal and civil courts show that breach of promise blighted countless lives, leaving a trail of misery out of all proportion to the wrong that the claim was supposed to be righting. The most common problem for unsuccessful defendants was debt, as breach of promise damages could be the financial ruin of a man. This was an unreasonable outcome to any claim, because damages were intended to compensate the plaintiff for the loss of her marriage to the defendant. If he could not afford to pay, then they were too high and the jury had overvalued any lifestyle advantage the woman would have obtained from being the defendant's wife. In addition to the damages, a man was usually faced with paying the plaintiff's legal bills as well as his own. It was not unknown for lawyers' costs to exceed the damages when a working-class man was the defendant and the jury had been restrained in the sum they awarded.

Until 1869, debtors' jails incarcerated men who were unable to pay the damages or legal fees and it was a legal maxim that a man who could not pay his dues with his pocket should do so with his person. In one such case, 68-year-old Richard Harrison appeared in the Insolvent Debtors Court in London in 1827, appealing for his liberty. He owed £150 for an unfulfilled promise to marry Mary Baker, a 69-year-old widow. In law, Harrison faced two years in jail for a breach of promise debt unless Mary agreed to his release and she would not. As the judges delved into the circumstances of his broken promise, they discovered that when Harrison proposed he was surviving on £40 a year charity from a sister who shared her modest annuity with him. He may have been hoping that by marrying Mary he could live off her money, as his decision to court another widow occurred when Mary's grandchildren threatened to put his brains out if he married their grandmother.

The judges reached the sensible conclusion that Harrison should have his freedom, as Mary would not have improved her own lifestyle if they had married. The case begs the question of why the jury awarded anything other than token damages against a man who had no assets or income of his own, although the press report of the breach of promise trial shows that Mary's witnesses painted a good view of his finances.

When imprisonment for debt was abolished, bankruptcy was the only option for obtaining the damages awarded by the court if the man did not pay. A gentleman usually applied for his own bankruptcy. If he did not, he demonstrated that he had no intention of paying and his creditors could ask the court to appoint someone to manage his financial affairs. Bankruptcy courts dealt with applications from a number of respectable men whose only debt was incurred through the breach of promise claim. Amongst them were a surprising number of army officers, which suggests that when the purchase of regimental commissions was abolished in 1871 and military promotion was based on merit, juries failed to appreciate that young officers were not wealthy men of fortune.

The risk of high damages led to male defendants trying to conceal their assets before the case came to court, perhaps transferring property to a relative or selling it at a very low value within the family. If property could be hidden successfully, then filing for bankruptcy was a way of frustrating the jury. There was a working assumption that a bankrupt should pay a third of his debts before he was discharged and judges had to tread a fine line to avoid releasing the man from his obligations too easily and not leaving him with a millstone around his neck for life. In 1921, Harry Taylor from Blackburn was released from a 17-year bankruptcy on condition that he paid £75 to the woman he jilted in 1904, who had never received a penny of her £224 award.

From a modern viewpoint it is easy to dismiss parental disapproval of cross-class romances in the nineteenth century as snobbery, but this misjudges the very real problems a young man's impetuous offer of marriage might create for his family. Most young men were not 'in a condition to regard an extra expenditure of some one or two hundred pounds', as 'a matter of trifling moment'. When a young man could not afford the damages awarded to the woman he had let down, his parents might feel obliged to pay them so that he avoided bankruptcy and its attendant social disgrace, perhaps to the detriment of his sister's marriage settlement.

If a young man's savings were swallowed up, it could take many years before he was in a position to maintain a wife and family, and if he never managed to build up any capital of his own he might be forced to remain an impoverished bachelor for the rest of his life. There are examples of fathers who left their son only a life interest in the fortune they had built up to protect family wealth from breach of promise claims.

Working-class men were in a more difficult position than their middle-class contemporaries, because they rarely had more than a few pounds to buy their way out of an engagement and spurned women could make very unrealistic demands. Poor men often had to pay damages by instalments, and in 1886, when a young bookkeeper's offer to pay a shilling a week was sanctioned by the court, the arrangement meant that it would take him 30 years to clear damages of £40 and legal costs of a similar amount; an unsatisfactory situation for defendant and plaintiff.

A more insidious debt was incurred by William Ellis who was told to pay Crewe publican, Susannah Walley, £500 in 1894, after the jury believed her claim that Ellis was a wealthy man; something that he vigorously denied. Reports of the hearing reveal that Susannah was young, attractive, vivacious – and vindictive. She openly admitted in the witness box that she had brought the case to punish Ellis and the jury's reasons for assessing her loss so highly seem very questionable. Ellis's description of his means must have been more accurate because a debt court allowed him to pay her £2 a month.

In 1896, Susannah took out a summons in the County Court

when Ellis defaulted on three instalments. He was instructed to pay the £6 arrears or spend a month in prison and warned that he would be dealt with harshly if he defaulted again. Ellis placed on record the fact that Susannah had married six months after winning her damages and suffered no detriment by not being married to him, but to no avail. The County Court had no remit to consider the circumstances in which the debt had arisen. Men who paid damages by instalments were too poor to appeal about the reasonableness of their situation, so senior judges were never obliged to address whether damages that would take more than 20 years to pay off were acceptable outcomes to breach of promise cases.

Claims involving women like Susannah, who ruthlessly pursued a man for money he did not have, provide powerful evidence that two wrongs do not make a right. Rather than being too critical of a woman determined to extract her money, or even of a man trying to hide his assets, lawyers and jurors should be held partially responsible for this bad behaviour. Expressing outrage or sympathy for a woman with a high award of damages was pointless if it overestimated what the man could pay. Not only did the woman have to come to terms with not being married, she then had to come to terms with not receiving the compensation she expected.

Occasionally, the outcome of a breach of promise claim was more serious than a long-term debt. Frederick Mayell had the full support of his new wife's family when Miss Roberts sued him in 1899. She accepted £40 and Mayell's father-in-law told him to take his wife away for a holiday and that he would settle the payment. Despite the advantages of a low settlement, and family support, the claim preyed on Mayell's mind and three days later he arrived at Hatton Asylum in Warwickshire, only to be turned away. The following morning he was found dead in bed after cutting his throat.

A year later, Squire Green, the 25-year-old son of a Leeds nurseryman, did not appear in court or send a lawyer to represent him, so Harriet Gray's version of their broken engagement went unchallenged. It seems probable that lack of money prevented Green from obtaining legal advice on how to deal with the claim, as he ignored an offer to settle for £100, a reasonable sum given the pair's status in life. Harriet's lawyer branded Green as a disreputable young man who had seduced Harriet during their eight-year engagement and then abandoned her when he met someone else shortly before the wedding. An outraged jury awarded her £350. When Green discovered the verdict he went to his father's shop and hanged himself.

***

Breach of promise could be exploited by the unscrupulous. The claim posed an especially serious problem for people with impaired mental capacity because the law focussed on the fact of a proposal and held defendants responsible for their promises. However, in some cases involving men with mental illnesses or learning disabilities their condition must have been clearly apparent to the plaintiff when the proposal was made. Some women had deliberately enticed a vulnerable man into offering marriage. In 1905, Alfred Kemp's counsel argued that Florence Cunningham had all but ordered his client to propose, knowing that he was easily led and had already been obliged to settle two other breach of promise claims. Her scheming was not quite as lucrative as she had hoped. After rejecting £750 to settle the claim informally she obtained only £500 damages from the jury.

Vulnerable women could also find themselves targets for extortion. Ann Crellin, a 40-year-old spinster, appears to have been lonely and naïve when she accepted a proposal from John McGill in 1841, though she had sufficient wit to insist on protecting her assets with a marriage settlement in her favour. McGill then refused to marry her unless she settled her property on him and threatened to sue for half her fortune, claiming that she had broken her promise to become his wife. He demanded £250 to release her from their engagement, which she paid before advisors told her that he had no grounds to bring a claim. When McGill was arrested for extortion, investigations revealed that he was a married man.

There is evidence that numerous women were involved in extortion cases. Some were opportunists who exploited an unexpected situation; others were career criminals who schemed to entrap a man into an indiscreet proposal so that they could threaten to bring a claim. From 1870, there are many contemporary indications that blackmail was widespread and it seems probable that droves of men and some women came to private arrangements under threat of court proceedings, with the associated costs, inconvenience, publicity and risk that an unaffordable award would be made against them. One vicar, fearful for his public reputation, settled a false claim by paying £60 rather than become embroiled in a court battle.

Most blackmail was probably low-level opportunist mischief that could be bought off for a few pounds, but professional extortioners used the threat of a spurious claim to intimidate wealthy men. In 1889, Amelia Demay and Charles Grand, a pair of French criminals living in London, were convicted at the Old Bailey for conspiring to extort money from Malcolm Morris, a Harley Street surgeon. Amelia had claimed damages of £2,000 for his breach of promise, which she alleged had been made in the first floor front sitting room of her lodgings in 1886, and that Morris had breached it by withdrawing himself from her society. It is unclear why Morris was targeted. He said he had been picked out after visiting a patient who lodged at the boarding house Amelia ran.

It is possible that he came to the couple's attention for a different reason. *The Observer* once noted that: 'London is a very small place, and that unless a man has more than usual sagacity, his follies and weaknesses are, sooner or later, sure to find him out'.

Grand rented an office in The Strand from where he allegedly watched for married men in the company of fast women, discovered who they were and then wrote to them stating that an action of a serious nature would be commenced against them, unless they came to some arrangement to prevent this. As part of the plan to extort money from Morris, Grand tried to bribe a porter named Alfred Walker to give false evidence in a breach of promise case by identifying Amelia and Morris as a lady and gentleman he had seen walking arm in arm. Walker, who considered that the risk of five years' penal servitude was not covered by the £10 he was offered, declined to assist. Amelia also tried to buy witnesses to support her claim. Grand was jailed for two years and Amelia for 18 months, both with hard labour.

At the turn of the century, some commentators believed that

many women lied under oath about promises of marriage and that the law turned a blind eye. When Sophia Watson, a five-times convicted fraudster, alleged that Major General Henry Fitzhugh fell for her whilst she was in prison, the law did not ignore her false evidence, even though her £10,000 claim was dismissed by the jury and she did not profit from her lies. In 1904, she was convicted of criminal perjury and received a jail sentence of four years with hard labour. It is impossible to conclude whether action was taken against her because she had a criminal record or because Fitzhugh was a member of the establishment. The misery of extortion, although unpleasant, could be faced down if a man had resources available.

Poor men were often powerless when confronted with a breach of promise claim. From the mid-1870s, when manual and unskilled workers began to find themselves threatened with court action, their restricted options could lead to lifelong domestic misery, and sometimes crime. When a fiancé hesitated about committing to marriage, an ugly sub-culture developed whereby a woman hinted that she would take advice about her legal rights unless the man named the day. Minnie Sayer wrote to tell Robert Fuller that she was planning to see a solicitor when he began to avoid her.

Some men responded to the threat by agreeing to arrange the wedding. This seems a degrading way for a woman to secure a husband, but impoverished women were not necessarily hoping for a marriage made in heaven. The low wages, drudgery and insecurity of jobs that unskilled and poorly educated women could obtain, made many keen to swap paid work for the married state, even with a reluctant partner. Being the angel in the house for their penniless soul-mate was less desirable for poor women than a loveless union with a man who could provide for them.

Some marriages arranged after the threat of a breach of promise claim ended in divorce, often with the wife deserted within months of the wedding. In 1890 Elizabeth Smith decided to bring a claim against Richard Cartwright with whom she had walked out for several months. Faced with this the two families conferred and devised a way to finance the couple's life together. They married and Elizabeth became pregnant, but within weeks Cartwright deserted her and began to cohabit with Emmie Spilman. In March

1893, Elizabeth obtained a divorce. Later that year Cartwright and Emmie were married. Happily, Elizabeth also attracted another suitor and remarried in 1897.

A few men about to face a breach of promise claim resorted to desperate measures. In 1886, London barman, John Reynolds, was sentenced to 20 years' penal servitude for trying to poison his wife, Sarah. Reynolds had unwisely proposed to another woman and, faced with committing bigamy or a ruinous claim for breach of promise, he made an amateur attempt to solve his dilemma by handing Sarah a drink laced with sulphate of copper. Noticing small crystals in the bottom of the cup, Sarah made herself vomit and appears to have suffered no lasting effects. In 1920, brickyard manager William Cook tried to kill his wife and himself to escape a miserable marriage. Rather than pay the £150 damages awarded by a jury for refusing to set a wedding date, he decided to marry. Three months later he struck his wife many times around the head with a hammer before trying to cut his throat with a razor. The couple were discovered alive but seriously injured and Cook faced criminal charges for his actions.

The sad aftermaths of a number of breach of promise cases merited only the briefest notice in the newspapers of the day and were never included in the limited debate about whether the claim ought to be reformed or abolished. Its role in crimes of violence, and as a weapon of revenge was not apparent, and it seems likely that innumerable men, and the women who coerced them into honouring a regretted promise, lived miserable and lonely lives behind the respectable facade of a loveless marriage. Only one tragic, but atypical, case achieved wide public attention when Catherine Kempshall's fury at losing a breach of promise claim against Edgar Holland led to one of the most sensational crimes of the 1890s.

Catherine Kempshall was born in Sussex in 1864 and moved to London in her late teens. Aged 20, she earned a precarious living as a chorus girl in the theatre, supplemented by occasional prostitution for wealthy admirers. Nothing is known of her stage career other than that she had a singing part in *A Trip to the Moon*, at Her Majesty's Theatre, and it seems unlikely that she was a talented actress. In 1885, she met Edgar Holland, a wealthy businessman from the Wirral. His fortune at that time was probably in the region of £100,000. Aged 37, he was almost twice her age, a bachelor and a man of the world. The pair appear to have met casually in Bond Street, an area known for high-class prostitutes, and went off to a hotel in the Haymarket.

Catherine was a strikingly attractive young woman, tall with delicate features and abundant golden hair that tumbled down her back. Holland, who concealed his true identity behind the alias of Henry Lancaster when frequenting prostitutes, was very strongly attracted by her. Shortly after they met he arranged for his London solicitors to pay off his existing mistress in the capital and asked Catherine to leave the stage and move into rooms that he would take for her, so that they could live together when he came to London. Catherine maintained that the arrangements to establish her as Holland's mistress also included his offer of marriage, one that he allegedly repeated three or four times during the first years of their relationship.

Their early years are shadowy but appear to have been happy. Holland rented rooms in Gower Street, which were owned by Bessie Wells and the pair lived together as Mr and Mrs West when he was in London. They also took holidays together and, according to Catherine, Holland encouraged her to study languages to improve herself, gave her an allowance of £150 a year and also rented fashionable rooms for her in Liverpool. What Holland did not do was to take her across the Mersey to his Wirral home or introduce her to his family. There seems no doubt that he only ever regarded her as a mistress, but breach of promise was based on whether a man ever offered a woman marriage, not whether he genuinely intended to make her his wife.

By 1892, an estrangement had developed between the couple. The reasons were not recorded but might relate to Catherine's mental health. It seems possible that she began to display symptoms of a condition that would now be diagnosed as a form of schizophrenia around this time. By spring 1894, the relationship had collapsed. In autumn 1894, Catherine brought a claim for breach of promise, requesting damages of £10,000, the sum she said that Holland had promised to settle on her when they married.

The case reached court in January 1895 and was settled minutes before the jury were due to hear it. Holland denied any promise, though he offered a generous settlement of £1,000 and £200 legal costs so that his former mistress could live a respectable life. Her barrister persuaded her to agree to this but omitted to mention the three conditions stipulated by Holland; the court records were to show a verdict for the defendant, and Catherine had to return all his letters and agree not to molest him.

When Catherine discovered the additional conditions her fury knew no bounds. A few days later she went to the Appeal Court asking for the settlement to be set aside and the case heard by a jury. The appeal judges decided that Catherine could not be bound by conditions she had not agreed to, though, as the Master of the Rolls pointed out to her, Holland's offer was a very advantageous one and that in a case settled by agreement, entering judgement was a formality and did not mean that the case had been decided against her.

From this point, Catherine voiced an intense suspicion of all lawyers, considering them dishonest and corrupt. It seems probable this hatred stemmed from her barrister and solicitor withdrawing their services because she could not pay her legal bills. By spring 1895, Catherine was actively managing the preparations for the hearing, evidenced by a curious episode when she was charged with smashing the windows of her former solicitor in an unsuccessful attempt to recover her paperwork. She always claimed that her former solicitor held a letter from Holland which referred to a promise of marriage. It is possible that a solicitor may have retained such a significant letter as a surety if his fees had not been paid and this tends to suggest that Holland had proposed.

One afternoon in June 1895, Catherine made her way to Putney Heath and loitered on the street where Holland's married sister, Emily Carlisle lived. When Emily returned home, Catherine rushed towards her carriage, pulled out a revolver and fired through the window, narrowly missing Emily's head. Catherine was immediately arrested, charged with attempted murder and sent to Holloway Gaol to await trial. As the breach of promise case was heard before the criminal trial, Catherine struggled under several disadvantages. Prison was not the best place to prepare a case and a woman arriving from prison in charge of a wardress to present it was unlikely to make a good impression on a jury, however attractive she was. Lack of precision about which of Holland's many letters referred to marriage also damaged her case, as the judge refused to let her read them out speculatively.

Catherine had two witnesses to support her claim: her brother Albert who stated that Holland had told him in 1886 that he intended to marry Catherine; and Bessie Wells, the landlady from Gower Street, who had initially believed that Mr and Mrs West were a married couple. Bessie indicated that when she discovered her own mistake, Holland explained that Catherine incorrectly thought that he intended to marry her. Bessie also revealed that when Catherine brought her case Holland called to see her and said there was no promise. This visit was not presented in court as an overt attempt to buy off a witness, but Bessie may have toned down her evidence as a result of it. Albert Kempshall had also been asked to meet Holland's solicitors.

Highly emotional and devoid of legal experience, Catherine then ruined her fragile case. She called Holland to the witness box and asked him whether he had promised to marry her. He firmly denied any promise, at which point the foreman of the jury told the judge there was no case to answer. The jury's decision provoked a violent and angry response from Catherine, who leapt towards Holland, screaming that he was a liar. It took two prison staff to restrain her and remove her from the courtroom and almost an hour before she was calm enough to leave the building.

That afternoon she appeared at the Old Bailey to answer the charge of attempting to murder Emily Carlisle. Catherine must have been articulate and persuasive because, representing herself, she convinced the jury to acquit her of that charge and the lesser one of grievous bodily harm. Catherine explained that she fired the gun to get herself arrested so that she could place her grievances about Holland before the public. Before he discharged her from custody, the judge pointed out that the sentence for attempted murder was life imprisonment with penal servitude and advised her not to let her supposed grievances influence her temper in the future.

Determined to prove that she had been cruelly used, Catherine spent the rest of the year bringing unsuccessful appeals to court, trying to obtain a retrial of her claim against Holland and to recover the letter allegedly evidencing his promise of marriage from her former solicitor's executors. On 23 December she pleaded guilty to assaulting Joseph Broughton, a clerk employed by Holland's solicitors. The slap across his face followed two months of verbal aggression and threats by Catherine against Holland and his solicitors, who were now trying to negotiate an informal settlement with her. Holland had offered to pay £300 and an allowance of £100 a year, which was more advantageous than the £1,000 she had refused.

The assault charge may have been brought to stop the nuisance Catherine was creating. She spent Christmas and New Year in prison, after being told to find a surety of £50 to guarantee her good behaviour for six months or spend two weeks behind bars. It is unclear how she spent the early months of 1896, or how she managed to live on her dwindling resources. She reinterpreted her grievance against Holland and began to tell strangers that she was an heiress cheated out of a fortune by her guardian's lies. In August she travelled north and arrived unexpectedly at Holland's home. In a long, private interview he promised to do something for her by the end of September and gave her some money so that she could return to Sussex. He then set off for a holiday in Europe.

During September, Catherine bombarded his home and office with letters and receiving no answer, returned to Liverpool where she took lodgings, visited his home and offices and wrote several letters to his solicitor demanding to know when he would return. She was also pouring out her hatred of an unnamed man to strangers and threatening to kill him.

Holland returned from his seven-week holiday on 26 October and must have been greeted with lurid accounts about Catherine from his housekeeper, office staff and James Alsop, his Liverpool solicitor. He immediately wrote to Catherine, telling her to go back to London and instruct a lawyer as his London solicitors were dealing with the matter. He offered to meet her at his offices on 29 October if she wanted him to explain his plans and asked Alsop to witness the meeting.

The two men were sat on one side of a long table and Catherine chose to stand, her cloak flowing round her. Holland began to explain that he would provide for her if she agreed that she had no legal or moral claim on him, returned his letters and stopped pestering him, his family and his advisors. Catherine interrupted with angry tirades about his cruelty towards her and reminded him of his promise. "You know I never promised to marry you", Holland replied. "I never wronged you. I have always treated you with kindness".

Catherine's self control snapped. She shouted, "you haven't, you beast", drew her hand from underneath her cloak and brandished a revolver. Before either man could react, she aimed at Holland's chest and then fired three further shots as Alsop rushed round the table, dashed her right arm down and put his own arm round her to pin her arms to her sides. Not realising that he was wounded, Holland moved round the table and helped to restrain her, whilst Alsop edged towards the door, still clutching Catherine's hand and shouted for help. As staff raced in to assist, Holland collapsed onto the table and Catherine seated herself in a chair and fell silent, observing his distress. When a policeman arrived the last words she heard Holland moan were, "take that woman away. I cannot bear the sight of her".

Only the bullet that hit Holland's chest caused serious injury and an emergency operation removed it from his lung a few hours later. He had a strong constitution and initially he began to rally until he contracted pneumonia. From that point his condition deteriorated and he died on 11 November 1896.

As soon as Catherine was arrested her state of mind attracted attention and prison staff requested an immediate assessment of her mental condition, as did the solicitor she appointed to act for her. When the police took statements from people who had spoken to her in Liverpool it became apparent that she was a very sick woman. When she stood trial for Holland's murder in March 1897, the jury concluded that, despite illness, Catherine had known what she was doing. They convicted her of murder, though with a recommendation for clemency. The judge passed the death sentence but her solicitor submitted a plea to the Home Office for a reprieve.

A public petition for mercy soon collected 17,796 signatures and members of Holland's family were supportive of it. At that time, decisions were made with little delay and 11 days later the Home

Office announced that because of her medical condition she had been reprieved and would be transferred to Broadmoor Criminal Lunatic Asylum, as the hospital was then known.

Two days later, Catherine travelled by train and carriage to Broadmoor, accompanied by a prison warder and wardress, calm and wearing her own clothes, presumably the dark dress, short dark cape, black straw hat with a white band and short veil she had worn at her trial. As the gates shut behind her, Catherine Kempshall disappeared from public view until 1952, when a short paragraph in *The Guardian* stated that:

> *a verdict of death by natural causes was returned at Broadmoor Institution yesterday on Miss Catherine Kempshall, aged 88, who had been detained there for nearly 55 years. She was one of the oldest patients. Miss Kempshall was found guilty at Liverpool Assizes in 1897 of the murder of a man friend and sentenced to death. Later she was certified as insane and sent to Broadmoor.*

Catherine always maintained that she was a wronged woman, and whether or not Holland had ever proposed was a secret he took to his early grave. To their contemporaries, Catherine's wild outbursts and threats seemed evidence in themselves that a man like Holland would never have offered marriage to her. Yet it is plausible that Catherine was telling the truth. There are similarities between her situation and other claims brought against wealthy men by working-class women who spoke of entering into a sexual relationship because of a promise of marriage, but were unable to produce any corroborating evidence.

As a successful businessman Holland was probably used to getting his own way. Paying off his existing mistress shows that he was determined to have Catherine. It seems feasible that he did promise marriage to secure her agreement and repeated it to keep her happy early in the relationship if she questioned his sincerity. Holland would have expected that he could buy his way out of any promise he made. Most women of Catherine's background would have been delighted to accept £1,000.

The three senior judges who refused Catherine's appeal for a second trial may have believed her, as they emphasised that she had ruined her case with mistakes that no experienced barrister would have made and suggested that Holland's denial of a promise under oath might not necessarily have weighed as heavily with them as it did with the jury.

Catherine was prone to detecting conspiracy where none existed, but she does not appear to have been a dishonest or untruthful woman and she never attempted to conceal discreditable episodes in her life, such as her youthful involvement in prostitution. Some of her apparently fanciful allegations about Holland were confirmed by his solicitors, who acknowledged using private detectives in connection with the breach of promise case and contacting Catherine's witnesses. This begs the question of whether members of her own legal team were approached.

Holland was exonerated by the jury and had no need to do anything for a former mistress who had become impossible to deal with, yet he was prepared to increase his financial inducement to secure her signature on a document confirming that he never offered her marriage. Perhaps he knew that one of his letters had referred to marriage and was unable to discover what had happened to it.

An expert barrister with two witnesses and the missing letter might have persuaded a jury that Holland had breached a promise. How Catherine would have reacted to winning the case is unknowable, but it seems unlikely that she would have been satisfied with her damages. Holland's rejected offer of £1,000 (currently worth £111,000) was, as the Master of the Rolls explained, very generous in the context of damages being awarded at that time. Unfortunately, she did not understand that her demand for £10,000 was a pipe dream. Juries would not award exemplary damages against a wealthy man who had lied to a lower-class woman of dubious virtue.

In 1879, MP Farrar Hershell described the unpalatable aspects of breach of promise which had been identified when he tried to interest Parliament in reforming the claim. As it offered redress to women who were seduced under a promise of marriage it was not considered appropriate to remove this remedy from them. In 1885, Parliament began to address the problems of prostitution and the exploitation of young girls and gave females who had been enticed into prostitution the right to sue their seducer for damages. Forward thinkers might have wondered whether giving women seduced under a promise of marriage a similar right of redress could be the first step in tackling the unsavoury aspects of breach of promise, but the idea was not articulated and the opportunity slipped away unnoticed.

The negative consequences of breach of promise intensified from the mid 1880s, as the claim plummeted down the social scale and drew working men into its jaws. For the next 80 years their lives were blighted, perhaps less by an actual claim than by the threat of one. It is a sad reflection on the country's law-makers that they were prepared to condone a claim of misery, vengeance and extortion until the swinging sixties.

It is a tribute to the sense and maturity of many women that they were prepared to forgo the right to wreak havoc on a man if he realised that his promise to marry had been a mistake, and allowed breach of promise to wither on the vine. As MP Edith Summerskill observed in 1943, 'the modern woman, far from demanding damages, thanks her lucky stars that she has learned the worth of her man before marriage and not after'.

Chapter 9

THE REAL MISS HAVISHAMS
THE MYTHS AND REALITIES OF BREACH OF PROMISE

The woman wished to enter into a solemn engagement with as little precaution as she would use in taking a week's lodgings.
(Mr Justice Bramwell, *The Times*, 20 April 1875)

Perhaps the most famous jilted bride is a work of fiction. In *Great Expectations*, Miss Havisham, an embittered, middle-aged spinster, haunts her family home for over 20 years as a spectre in faded bridal finery, presiding over a mouldering wedding feast and teaching her adopted daughter, Estella, to hurt and despise any man foolish enough to offer her his heart. To a contemporary audience, receiving a note from the bridegroom on the morning of the wedding, as was the young Miss Havisham's fate, was a credible way of accounting for her bitter hatred of the male sex and a dramatic device for drawing the reader into the fictional world created by Charles Dickens.

Breach of promise of marriage was always a theatrical piece of law, because damages were based as much on a jury's subjective judgements about both plaintiff and defendant as on any legal rules. This created an inherent uncertainty between a warring couple, which translated well to the stage and into fiction, helping to blur the distinction between real life and make-believe. Television drama has regularly featured either a bride or groom failing to turn up at the altar as one of its staple plots, to heighten the tension in a story.

In real life, less than one per cent of breach of promise plaintiffs had their hopes dashed on the wedding morning, or waited at the church or registry office for a man or woman who never arrived. A last-minute change of heart is one of the many misconceptions surrounding breach of promise. The reality of being jilted was very different, but equally sensational.

The earliest myth to attach itself to breach of promise originated in the eighteenth century. A key part of a middle-class female plaintiff's claim for damages was that she had been condemned to perpetual spinsterhood. Respectable men were said to refuse to consider proposing to a jilted woman, in case she was in some way responsible for her broken engagement. From the scant detail available about middle-class plaintiffs in the eighteenth century it is impossible to discover whether they did go on to marry, but it seems likely that the arguments made on this point were created by barristers, without any supporting evidence, to maximise the damages.

A woman's blighted hopes of matrimony were regularly spoken of in the court room from the 1790s until 1891, but by 1804 it was usually the judge who raised this when summing up for the jury. Judges generally stated that a woman's chances were appreciably diminished by a broken engagement, but they never clearly explained why, suggesting that this was just received wisdom rather than a proven disadvantage.

From the first decade of the nineteenth century to the last, there is strong evidence that some breach of promise plaintiffs did marry after the court case. For many of them too little personal information is known to be sure of identifying the correct woman in public records, but marriage indexes regularly contain brides with the same name as a plaintiff, in the area where she was living, a few years, or sometimes months after the breach of promise hearing. It is likely that some of these entries refer to women who had taken claims to court.

It was not necessary for a jilted woman to have an exemplary character for her to find a husband. Despite giving birth to an illegitimate son after her fiancé of two years decided not to honour his offer of marriage, it seems that Elizabeth Forster married in 1808, three years after winning her claim for damages. Five years after suing her former employer, virtuous governess Anne Lancey probably married Joseph Truelove in 1821. Mary Alice Orford, appears to have become Mrs Wilson in Liverpool, six years after receiving her record damages and unmarried teenage mother, Charlotte Daniel, may have wed Matthias Butler in 1828, two years after her scandalous elopement with Captain Bowles.

Actress Maria Foote captivated the Earl of Harrington with her beauty, and in 1831, became his Countess, despite her tainted past. She had borne Colonel William Berkeley two illegitimate children before receiving a proposal from a young landowner, Joseph Hayne, who later cited her bad character as the reason for breaking his word. Maria won her breach of promise case against him in 1824 and £3,000, arguing that Hayne had known about the birth status of her children when he proposed.

As the nineteenth century progressed, the likelihood of a woman receiving another offer began to be raised by the defence in an attempt to keep a woman's damages to a low level. The first recorded instance of this may be the claim made by Jemima Wright, which was heard at Stroud in 1827. The suggestion raised no eyebrows in court, nor comment in the press, indicating that the marriage of a previously jilted woman was neither novel nor newsworthy. In 1844, *The Observer* reported that Mrs Georgiana Dorey, who had recently been arrested for conspiracy to defraud the government, had as Miss Georgiana Richards, obtained £250 damages from Reverend Taylor in 1834. Even a failed plaintiff whose reputation was damaged by her claim could marry well. Mary Smith became the wife of a gentleman, despite incurring public odium in 1846 when she fabricated letters to make it seem that Earl Ferrers had proposed to her.

In the middle of the century, there were several successful breach of promise cases brought by 'artful and abandoned hussies' who falsely claimed to have received a proposal from a man of means, or had enticed them into making one, so that they could use the damages to set up home with a different man. Between 1851 and 1862, Amelia Harrison, Anne Hedge and Catherine Knights all married within a few months of winning their claim. In 1869, defence lawyers pointed out that accountant's daughter, Kate Fleming, might expect a husband as worthy and well-off as James Thompson, as her attractions were unimpaired.

John Marsh's lawyer observed that if Mary Lamb was as attractive as her two sisters who had given evidence, then she would have no difficulty in finding another, more worthy suitor. In 1873, the judge remarked that the £500 that Annie Hammond had accepted to settle her case might enable her to find a lover more faithful than Joseph Belton, who had jilted her for Eliza Williamson.

Clara Pilbeam was 21 when John Clemence broke their engagement in 1881. She married William Stevens, a solicitor's clerk, five years later. In their marriage licence and in censuses taken during Stevens's lifetime, three years have been subtracted from Clara's age, so that she only appeared to be two years older than her husband rather than five. The missing years reappear in the 1911 census when Clara was a widow. This may indicate that when Clara met her future husband, she was worried about her age. Unmarried women were considered to be on the shelf by the time they turned 25, and Stevens might also have thought the age-gap between them too great, as it was conventional for a man to be a little older than his wife.

In 1891, the marriage of Gladys Knowles was widely noted in the press. Her nuptials took place less than three months after the Appeal Court had confirmed how much Leslie Duncan should pay for refusing to honour their engagement. Gladys's wedding seems to have formed a landmark moment in breach of promise claims, particularly as the judges had stated that she would struggle to find a husband. After this point any argument about compensation for reduced prospects of marriage dissolves. Claims later in the decade began to refer to the fact that a plaintiff had already been courted by someone else. In the twentieth century there is ample evidence in marriage records that breach of promise plaintiffs found husbands.

Despite eighteenth century emphasis on a woman needing an unsullied reputation to secure a husband, all but the wealthiest men would have considered a bride with a few hundred pounds of her own more desirable than a poor one of unimpeachable character. A couple of hundred pounds was an excellent contribution towards setting up a respectable home with a working man, whilst women with a thousand pounds or more were very attractive to middle-class bachelors. Half the women who brought a claim for breach of promise sued a man of a higher social standing. The damages that they received would have maintained governesses and farmer's daughters in the marriage market, probably with men of their own social class.

An illegitimate child was not an insuperable barrier to finding a husband, if a woman had some money of her own. Amongst the working-classes, being seduced under a promise of marriage was not regarded as the same heinous crime it was to the middle-class. A self-employed working man might be happy to accept a child able to help in his shop or trade if it saved him the expense of having to employ an assistant.

Marrying a widow was not a social taboo and before the compulsory registration of births, marriages and deaths it was easy to adopt a different marital status. After receiving £300 from her first fiancé, Matilda Ubsdell arbitrarily changed her name to Matilda Black in 1845 and posed as a widow to disguise her son's illegitimacy. She received a proposal from a young railway clerk, who later discovered the deception and declined to marry her. Despite winning just one farthing from him, within two years Matilda had convinced John Symes to make an honest woman of her.

For a number of women who brought a claim for breach of promise, damages were not about being compensated for a broken heart and diminished chances of marriage. Some spinsters and widows already had an income from a business or a settlement and had not actively been seeking a husband when they received an offer of marriage. When proposals were regarded as business arrangements by both parties from the outset, pursuing a claim for compensation was just good business sense if the deal went wrong.

High mortality, especially in childbirth, produced an ever-replenishing supply of widowers, some of whom offered marriage as an alternative to employing a housekeeper to run the home or a nursemaid to look after the children. Elizabeth Tyndall's request for compensation was likened by Henry Short's barrister to a dispute about the wrongful dismissal of a housekeeper, rather than breach of promise of marriage, because of the businesslike tone both parties had adopted in their correspondence. When Annie Allan sued Walter Chivers in 1900, the judge commented that the engagement was so clearly a business arrangement that he wondered whether he ought to ask the commercial court to decide the damages.

The extent to which breach of promise plaintiffs subsequently married is unknown because it is difficult to identify many of them afterwards in records. Just as some marriages can be found, sometimes death records confirm that the woman died unwed. It is clear that a broken engagement did not automatically condemn a woman to eternal spinsterhood and if her damages made her a little richer this could attract other suitors. Money, combined with matters such as looks, personality and opportunity for meeting other men, was the very practical factor determining whether she would receive a second offer, if she still wished to become a wife.

***

By the mid-nineteenth century, many women believed that breach of promise protected loyal fiancées from long, and ultimately unproductive engagements by ensuring that the man who deserted them had to provide financial security for the solitary years ahead. This thought may have comforted a woman as she waited anxiously for her fiancé to reply to her unanswered letters, but it was a myth. The majority of failed engagements where a woman received substantial compensation had existed for months rather than years. Protection from long engagements was important to women because their marriageable years were few. A woman who had not secured a husband by her mid-twenties would struggle against the younger women who left the school-room each year. Compounding the problem of a socially-imposed window of opportunity to wed, was a more practical anxiety. Men were in short supply in the mid and late nineteenth century, and women knew that some of their number would never receive an offer of marriage. In a society that saw a woman's role as running a home rather than working outside it, the need to attract a husband was a constant concern for young women and their parents.

Amongst the prosperous middle-classes, the anxiety to be married meant that engagements were formed after very short periods of acquaintance, often when the couple had only met for a few hours at parties and balls. In such an artificial atmosphere it was easy to gain a mistaken impression of the other person and their values. It was not unusual for engagements to take place within a month of the first meeting and a number of breach of promise cases feature a man who had proposed too quickly, perhaps whilst away on holiday, and then realised that he had mistaken his feelings, or underestimated the expense of providing for a wife.

Judges were divided about whether making a mistake during a short courtship was acceptable mitigation for breaking an engagement. In

1878, the Lord Chief Justice commented that 'ten days is a long time to be exposed to the attractions of a charming young girl, especially when dancing with her.' In 1883, Mr Justice Grove took the opposite view about a fortnight's acquaintance between plaintiff and defendant, suggesting that 'it would be better for people sometimes, perhaps, if they were to "keep company" a little while before they became engaged, as the commoner people did'.

Despite Mr Justice Grove's approval of their courtships, poorer people were also liable to form ill-considered engagements. Although lower-middle-class and working-class people had more privacy to get to know each other, quick decisions were sometimes required. If a couple walked out together half a dozen times, a man might find himself being asked by the woman's relatives to declare his intentions. This was a useful means of preventing a woman from spending too much time on a man who had no serious interest in her, but it may also have scared off someone who wanted to take longer to decide. Pressure for a hasty commitment from a man sometimes led to a conditional promise, but the short-term advantage of being 'spoken for' was not necessarily a benefit to a woman if the pair had no idea when they would be able to afford marriage.

If the couple drifted apart or the man changed his mind, the prospect of a breach of promise claim gave him no incentive to be honest and set his fiancée free. Instead he would let the engagement drag on, hoping that the woman would find someone else and jilt him, or tire of waiting and ask for her freedom. A few men who had decided against marriage even tried to provoke their fiancée into ending the engagement. In 1899, Plaistow boilermaker, Henry Halkett, wrote to his intended, Emma Male, explaining that after a wild night out with the boys he had contracted venereal disease. Emma realised she was being tricked and sued for breach of promise, receiving £120 after a shame-faced Halkett admitted to the court that he did not have any infection and must have penned his letter whilst drunk.

In 50 per cent of cases the failed engagement was between a couple from different classes. When the romance involved a poor woman and a lower-middle class groom, the man was often criticised for his mercenary behaviour if he had married a richer bride and ample damages were usually claimed because of his selfish behaviour towards the woman he had jilted. In reality, not all men who married a richer woman were the cads they were made to appear in court. It is perfectly feasible that a man could afford to marry a woman with assets of her own but was not in a position to support a wife who could not bring money into the marriage.

A contribution from the bride's family towards setting up a home, and the prospect of income from the investments in her marriage settlement to balance the household budget might be needed before a bachelor dared to change his marital status. In a number of claims where a man had married a richer woman, the damages that the plaintiff received appear more like a slap on the wrist for the defendant, rather than substantial compensation for the woman he had jilted. The reason damages were not generous in these circumstances was that juries could only take into account the man's own resources, not those brought into the marriage by his new wife.

One measure of a long and ultimately unproductive engagement for a woman was when her fiancé married someone else. In the nineteenth century, this occurred in 26 per cent of breach of promise claims. The average damages awarded to women who had been abandoned for a different bride were £349, compared with £380 for those where another marriage was not involved. Ignoring awards of more than £1,000 gives a more realistic picture of what a lower-class woman might obtain and reveals that deserted women received on average 16 per cent less in damages.

Whatever the Victorians believed, the statistics show that women who had been engaged for several years did not receive substantial compensation for their loyalty, unless they had been in common-law marriages. A 60-year-old grocer, Margaret Blundell, received £35 when Peter Cropper deserted her after ten years to marry another woman, and Kate Fisher, aged 25, obtained only £50 from a surgeon after an engagement of five years. In the cases where a woman received good compensation for being jilted after a long engagement, jurors made a distinction between women who still had a realistic expectation of marriage at the point when the man changed his mind and those where it had long been obvious that the defendant had no intention of honouring his word.

Middle-class intellectuals launched a concerted attack on breach of promise in the 1870s, basing some of their criticisms on myth and presumption. One argument was that the damages women received were disproportionate to the injury suffered, with jurors being foolishly generous to undeserving plaintiffs. Critics of the action considered that any woman who was prepared to parade her feelings in a courtroom in order to obtain money deserved very little. The primary source of information for anyone who did not work in the legal profession was newspapers. By this time, the press had become very critical of women thought to have behaved badly and devoted column inches to denigrating supposed villainesses, whether they won or lost. In 1881, shortly after 39-year-old Kate Lamb, a solicitor's daughter won £1,000 from Arthur Fryer, a curate who was ten years her junior, *The Observer* drew attention to what it considered was a very weak claim ironically suggesting that:

> *action for breach of promise of marriage against a Dean or Archdeacon might possibly be permitted, but to curates a statutory protection should be granted similar to that which is accorded to undersized lobsters.*

A couple of years earlier, the paper had vented its wrath against Elizabeth Hall, who had unsuccessfully attempted to extort money from Demetrius Schillizzi with a breach of promise claim, pointing out that:

> *she was no guileless girl, but rather a very astute and experienced woman, able to reckon up the pecuniary value of a lover of the type of Mr Schillizzi, to recount every detail in her relationship with him, and, in the end, to put upon him a pressure which can hardly be described as gentle.*

Unusually the paper was also scathing of Schillizzi for his folly in not realising that a rich gentleman who accosted a comely widow in Regent Street, took her to the theatre and made her valuable presents might be running the risk of having some claim made against him. Men were often portrayed as victims, whilst their bad behaviour towards a plaintiff passed without public censure, even when the defendant had treated a woman disgracefully.

Newspaper readers were more likely to recall that the family of 19-year-old feather worker, Florence Joseph, were remorseless in their demands for compensation from a London bookmaker, and obtained £1,500, than that 19-year-old Hannah Wood, a poor farmer's daughter had been seduced by a rich manufacturer under a promise of marriage and received £350, after he cast her off, pregnant, saying that 'he'd had all he wanted from her'.

Sixty-four per cent of all women received no more than £200 in damages and the sum most usually awarded was £100. For working-class women who had been engaged for a couple of years or more and wasted money on wedding preparations, this level of compensation was not undeserved, so long as it was realistic for the man to pay it. The money, used wisely, would have brought them a little security, and was a reasonable outcome for those whose finances had been damaged by the man's inconsiderate behaviour. Mary Lamb had given up the prospect of an annual salary of £50 when she resigned her teaching post to please John Marsh. Commercial clerk, Arthur Pemberton, asked Violet Brice to give up her work as a waitress whilst he prepared their marital home, knowing that Violet's impoverished parents could ill afford to support her. When the home was ready he married Frances Gardner, offering Violet £10 compensation. The court awarded her £250.

What seems to have been at the root of the criticisms about over-generous juries was social class. Decent awards made to working-class women against middle-class men could create annoyance, unless the man had behaved exceptionally badly. Polly Frost was considered not to deserve the £200 Josiah Knight was told to pay her, because she was a servant and this represented over 20 times her annual salary. Knight tried unsuccessfully to appeal against damages that he considered excessive.

When Henry Joy was ordered to pay Elinor Miller £2,500, after his vindictive conduct destroyed her carefully nurtured business and prevented her from earning her own living, some critics thought that the sum was outrageous, given Elinor's murky past. In 1856, Eleanor Hewittson's lawyer summed up the views of the middle-classes towards poor women bringing claims for breach of promise, when he criticised Isaac Rowson's lawyer for arguing that Eleanor's family occupied a place in society that did not entitle them to the consideration that would be shown towards those of wealth or position.

The damages given to middle-class plaintiffs often seem more generous than those awarded to poorer ones, even when the defendant was of the same financial standing and the woman had suffered a similar loss. The most undeserving plaintiffs may have been young, middle-class women rather than working-class ones. Edith Barber, aged 18, Elizabeth Webster, 20, and Mary Mathiason, 21, all obtained damages of £2,000 or more, in cases without aggravating factors, after very short engagements, but this was rarely noticed by the action's middle-class critics. Perhaps the woman to profit most substantially from a short engagement was Sarah Miller, who received £350 after she had expected to become Abraham Moryjoseph's wife for just eight days.

Alongside the allegation that damages were usually too high, was the rhetoric that fraud and extortion were rife amongst breach of promise plaintiffs. A small number of claims were fabricated, but most of these appear to have been detected by juries which found for the defendant. A few others succeeded, only to be overturned on appeal. Rather than telling a blatant lie, several women were accused of entrapping a gullible man into a proposal so that they could sue for damages when he sought to free himself. Old men and callow youths were thought to be regular victims, as women sought damages from men they could not possibly have wanted for a husband.

Men under 24 represent ten per cent of unsuccessful defendants, and a similar proportion applies to men over 60. If young men were being exploited by worldly women then it seems likely that the women would be a few years older, but this was not the case. Men under 24 were usually sued by a woman of a similar age or younger, suggesting that these were relationships between equals, though occasionally a young man may have been set-up by the conniving parents of a girl of his own age. Beyond this, there is no evidence to suggest that young men were frequently the gullible victims of fraudulent women.

There is some evidence that old men may have been targeted for their money, usually by a woman of a similar age. Mature widows were often the butt of jokes in breach of promise theatricals and older spinsters were sometimes treated harshly by a jury. Both groups did badly when it came to damages, even if they won their claim. On average, women in their sixties obtained only £111 in damages and those in their fifties fared even worse with £91. Damages for women under 45 were much more generous; until this age they could hope to receive around £200. The difference does not seem to reflect life-expectancy, but contempt of some of the claims that older women brought in an effort to secure money for their old age. A few women tried to take advantage of defendants who suffered from dementia, whilst others had mistakenly thought the defendant was a man of means, only to discover that he had proposed for the same reason, believing that she could ensure him a comfortable old age.

Victorian marriages were usually formed with a man who was up to five years older than his bride. Breach of promise claims reveal that many failed engagements were between couples whose ages fell outside these parameters. Almost a third of plaintiffs were at least ten years younger than the defendant and over half these couples had an age gap of more than 20 years. For a woman, the attraction of a much older man appears to have been his social and financial standing, which was almost always higher than her own. Had the marriage taken place, the woman could have expected to increase her economic security and improve her standard of living.

A number of breach of promise plaintiffs were in their twenties and from the respectable working-class or the lower middle-class. They appear upwardly mobile in their ambitions. Defendants would have been considered men of means, by the plaintiff. Many were farmers, tradesmen with their own shop or craftsmen running their own business. As the nineteenth century progressed they were joined by men in regular employment. The uniting factor was that these men were believed to have resources at their disposal to pay damages, though this assumption was sometimes erroneous. Only one per cent of defendants were poor men who would have been living hand to mouth and these claims may have been acts of vengeance by a woman they had scorned.

A few engagements involved a very big age difference between the couple. Successful older men sometimes sought out a younger woman and some women considered it 'better to be an old man's darling than a young man's slave'. Whether there was mutual affection in these relationships is unclear, but a woman marrying an older husband would have expected a generous settlement for her anticipated widowhood. The greatest age difference between couples in breach of promise cases was between Sophia Darbon, the 31-year-old daughter of a wine cooper, and retired solicitor, Robert Rosser, who was 85. Sophia received £1,600 in 1841, which reflected Rosser's very substantial wealth.

The previous year, 30-year-old Eliza Hastings was awarded £100 when a sprightly doctor, Richard Ashley, aged 80, married someone else. In most cases involving age gaps of 20 years or more, the damages were not exceptional. Half the plaintiffs received no more than £200 and some reaped only the benefit of having their legal bills settled, as the damages were contemptuous. Jurors appear to have afforded some protection to old men if they thought that exploitation was involved, as they only awarded a substantial level of damages when it was clear that the man had been fully aware of the implications of his proposal and not pressured into making it.

***

Some underlying aspects of the breach of promise claim were not noticed by contemporary commentators. Comparing the damages awarded during the nineteenth century to women who worked for a living and those who did not, reveals that women in employment obtained an average of £261, whilst those who remained at home received £417. It was unusual for a woman who worked for her living to receive £1,000 in damages unless there were aggravating features to her claim. Women who did not work were twice as likely as a working woman to obtain at least £1,000.

Excluding awards of £1,000 or more identifies the experience of a more typical plaintiff, as it removes the effect of aggravating aspects and also eliminates the claims made by gentlemen's daughters against very wealthy men. The differential between the two groups still persists, with economically active women receiving £161, compared with £209 for those who did not work. The difference cannot be explained by the argument that working women were poor, and more likely to be suing men of limited resources. Working women were more likely to sue a man of better financial standing than their own than to sue a man without funds. Women who worked on a self-employed basis tended to obtain better damages than those who worked for wages, which may reflect approval of entrepreneurship, even by a woman, and willingness to compensate them for losses sustained in disposing of a business in preparation for marriage. Such women may also have had better opportunities to meet men outside their own class as a number sued men of a higher social standing.

Amongst the working women, one type of employment stands out as attracting higher damages: governesses, who received on average £439. This reflects the fact that most were respectable, middle-class ladies whose families could not afford to support them. Governesses were particularly susceptible to the effects of a tarnished reputation. The mere suspicion that a woman had behaved in a way that entitled a man to break his promise to marry her, could make it very difficult to find further employment in a society increasingly censorious of real or perceived impropriety. A similar sensibility to the effects of loss of reputation was shown in average damages of £376 awarded to nineteenth century teachers.

Although an irreproachable character was necessary for some women to be able to earn their living, critics of breach of promise sometimes mocked women who said they brought claims to establish their good character. They regarded this argument as a cover for more mercenary ambitions, querying why these women still accepted damages once their honour had been vindicated in public. The argument that the plaintiff wished to establish her character in public understandably featured more often in breach of promise claims after some women had used it successfully, but there is no indication that juries were more liberal with damages towards women who made this claim, unless it was necessary for a woman to vindicate her character before she could resume her occupation.

The effect of the awards to governesses and teachers means

that the compensation won by other working women for broken engagements was worth just two thirds of what was awarded to women who did not work. On average, they received £142, with ten per cent of them receiving a derisory sum of £10 or less. Some of these claims were attorney's actions which would have been better not brought, but a number indicate that women in some occupations were not highly regarded by the men who sat on juries. Women who ran boarding houses did very badly and those who worked in factories were rarely thought to merit substantial damages.

In contrast, the experiences of economically inactive women reveal that only five per cent received a derisory award, and many of them were the daughters of poor men. The Victorian middle-class ideal, to which most jurors would have subscribed, was that a woman's proper role in life was to remain at home and tend to domestic matters. Women who demonstrated that this type of socially acceptable occupation, rather than paid work outside the home, was their choice, were rewarded with levels of damages that allowed them some discretion about whether to try and earn a living. Half of these women obtained £200 or more, with 11 per cent receiving at least £1,000. Amongst the larger awards, the aggravating factors of pregnancy or poor conduct by the defendant were infrequent and some teenagers became very wealthy young women.

During the Edwardian era, the difference between the working and unoccupied persisted, though it is difficult to draw firm conclusions because newspaper reports provided much less detail about plaintiffs and defendants. Nevertheless, the highest awards continued to be made to women from genteel backgrounds and women in poorly-paid occupations infrequently received much compensation from a faithless fiancé. It raises the intriguing possibility that the decline of breach of promise claims in the early twentieth century was linked to the increase in female employment, and recognition by working women that reasonable damages for a broken engagement were not available.

Breach of promise is perhaps the only law that developed to give women a clear advantage over men, whether they were suing or being sued. Those who booked a date before the judge to substitute for a date before the vicar demonstrated that they were not passive creatures to be trampled over, but assertive women who were capable of protecting their own interests.

Chapter 10

In Want of a Wife?
Breach of Promise Cases pursued by Men

*A shilling is ordinarily the maximum damages a gentleman
suing a lady for inconstancy can expect.*
(Barnsley Independent, 3 September 1864)

Breach of promise law was not just about women seeking
compensation, as it also allowed a man who was jilted by a
woman to claim damages for her inconstancy. Few men chose
this course and it seems unlikely that men brought more than
two per cent of cases to court. All classes of society considered
a man who shamed a woman for breaking their engagement as
ungentlemanly. A sensible man allowed a woman to change her
mind, saving his own honour, if necessary, with the fiction that the
couple had parted by mutual agreement.

Victorian sentimentality about love and marriage coincided
with the decades when surplus females were abundant, so a
woman receiving an offer from a man with a broken engagement
to his name would not be unduly concerned if this was based on
the mature and sober realisation of both parties that they were not
made for each other.

The surplus of women of marriageable age provided men with
a wide choice of potential partners and single men who possessed
the means to support a wife did not need to remain unmarried
except by choice. If he found it difficult to meet suitable women,
then a man could advertise for a wife, reply to an advertisement
placed by a woman seeking a husband, or employ the services of
a matrimonial agency. He could also look outside his class to a
woman of a lesser social standing without losing respectability,
especially if she could bring money into the marriage.

Breach of promise cases involving male plaintiffs occurred

in every decade from the 1780s until the 1920s. As the highly mannered eighteenth century turned into the industrious nineteenth, spurned men very occasionally received token damages of up to £20 from a woman who, they claimed, had trifled with their feelings or rendered them an object of scorn and derision in polite society. It was hardly a sum to concern a wealthy woman having second thoughts about her fiancé. Women who were not wealthy were not sued for inconstancy. For a man as for a woman, breach of promise was about lost prospects, not lost love.

Barristers at this time often referred to juries at some unspecified place and time having awarded a jilted man a significant sum but there is scant evidence of large awards against a woman, other than where a man had incurred substantial expenditure preparing for the marriage and she had changed her mind without an adequate reason. Even then, the damages only compensated him for his outgoings. In 1803, Lord Ellenborough, summing up the case of Leeds v Cook, stated that 'there might be cases where even a man was entitled to large compensation', indicating that barristers indulged in highly exaggerated oratory on behalf of their male clients.

The last man to receive damages for being rendered an object of public ridicule was naval lieutenant Thomas Seymour, who won £2 (currently worth £215) when Lucy Garside, a rich young widow, ended their engagement of a few days' duration in 1822. The case was heard in the spa town of Bath, famed for its genteel social activities, rather than in one of the thrusting commercial centres where a mannered lifestyle was less important to the majority of people living there. This probably explains why Seymour thought that an archaic argument might net him a fortune.

Breach of promise claims against women were at their most numerous between 1821-24, when at least eight were heard in English courts. This parallels the surge of cases brought by women at this time. Male plaintiffs may have been encouraged by the success of John Pizzey in 1821 against Sarah Boulter, a former house servant. Pizzey and Sarah were engaged when she won £833 in a lottery. Rather than setting up home with the young coachman, Sarah used the money to secure herself a wealthier husband and accepted a proposal from John Boulter, who owned a painting and glazing business in Datchet. Pizzey, who was awarded £200, seemed genuinely upset by the loss of Sarah's affections, as well as the loss of a better lifestyle with her.

Sarah Boulter appears to be the only woman who was penalised in a breach of promise claim for poor conduct towards a man. From the 1830s, judges firmly emphasised that a man had suffered no damage unless he spent money on preparing for the wedding and told juries to ignore the loss of any capital or income the woman would have brought to the marriage, and claims for hurt feelings. Jilted men were considered capable of making their own way in life and of finding another bride.

The men who chose to drag their former fiancées before a jury shared three motivations: money, honour and revenge. They were not mutually exclusive. Money was by far the most common and was the key reason for more than 80 per cent of male plaintiffs bringing their case. In around a quarter of these the man, usually of more limited means than the woman, had spent a substantial sum preparing for married life. In 1871, George Currie was awarded £250 from his wealthy cousin, Mary Currie. Whilst he was buying and furnishing a house in London she was swept off her feet by a handsome Spaniard and broke her engagement, entering into a whirlwind marriage with this more exotic suitor.

Three quarters of those motivated by a woman's money were fortune-hunters who had targeted the woman for her wealth. Some selected as victims women who appeared to have no-one to protect their interests. Around 60 per cent of all fortune-hunters brought speculative claims when the woman married, probably hoping to achieve a private settlement from the newly-married couple. Lawyers regularly branded such plaintiffs as scoundrels who were 'attempting to pick the pockets' of hard-working and respectable people.

When a man sued a married woman he brought the case against the husband and wife jointly. Until the late-nineteenth century the law considered a husband and wife as a single legal personality and held a man answerable for the misdeeds of his wife. Although by 1800 making a man accountable for assaults and libels committed by his wife was viewed by some as unfair, it was still regarded as acceptable to hold a husband to account for his wife's broken promise to marry someone else. The rationale was that the husband had derived benefit, usually financial, from her perfidy.

A typical scoundrel's claim was made in 1793 by landscape gardener Charles Sands, who requested substantial damages from London haberdasher John Sayer and his wife Ann. She had recently inherited a fortune from her uncle, a retired coach builder, and, according to Sands, had promised to marry him after her uncle's death. Sands' lawyer argued that Sayer was as culpable as Ann for the broken promise, because he knew of Ann's engagement but still chose to court and then marry another man's fiancée. The jury were invited to award £2,500, the sum alleged to have been given by a jury hearing a similar case. Despite his lawyer's impassioned rhetoric, Sands provided no evidence that Ann had ever agreed to be his wife and was forced to withdraw his claim.

Young women who had already inherited property or who had a wealthy father to provide a substantial marriage settlement were magnets for fortune-hunters, but these cads did not restrict themselves exclusively to women with a large fortune or expectations. A girl such as Anne Ismay, who had a small annual income to take into marriage, was a very attractive prospect for William Hobson, who had no resources of his own. Anne broke her engagement in 1823 on the advice of an uncle, who identified that Hobson could not support a wife. She was told to pay him £50, which was surprising generosity by the jury.

Despite their efforts, fortune-hunters only succeeded in about half the cases they brought. Women tended to receive the benefit of the slightest doubt and several convinced the jury that an engagement had never existed, was conditional, or had been ended by the defendant. When a jury had to conclude that a woman had broken her promise, jurors countered the man's victory by awarding contemptuous damages of a farthing. A few juries were more liberal and awarded a shilling, which would have bought a couple of mugs of ale to toast the triumph. Following on from the jury's contemptuous award, most judges refused to order a woman to pay the man's legal fees, obliging him to settle the costs of his own case. Hitting fortune-hunters in the wallet quickly discouraged men from bringing claims.

Some women lost a case brought by a fortune-hunter by not understanding when they were entitled to end their engagement. In 1803, Elizabeth Cardinal eloped to take her vows to Charles Cook, rather than explain to William Leeds why she had changed her mind about marrying him. Leeds' behaviour had deteriorated as soon as her family's contribution to Elizabeth's marriage settlement had been agreed to his satisfaction. He threatened her with violence, attempted to seduce the wife of her father's bailiff and consorted with a lady of easy virtue on an overnight stay in London with her scandalised father. She was told to pay him one shilling in damages. If she had written to Leeds stating that she was not prepared to marry a man of his character, rather than to apologise for ending their engagement, Elizabeth would not have been considered to have broken her promise to become his wife.

In 1837, William Delves concealed his many vices from Mary Ann Holder and her family until his clumsy attempt to have Mary Ann's secure investments transferred into something more risky prompted her father to institute detailed enquiries into his background. This produced the unwelcome news that he had twice been in court as an insolvent debtor, had a violent temper and was a drunkard and a liar who portrayed himself as wealthier than he was.

A letter written to Delves by Mary Ann, a seemingly sensible woman of 32, was read in court. She revealed that Delves was her first and would be her last and only love and stated that she would prefer death than to be told by the one she loved that it was the paltry sum accompanying her that induced him to make the offer for her hand. Her words give a poignant insight into the pain of a mature and intelligent woman duped by a suitor who identified her fortune, and then endeavoured to visit the same places that she did until he managed to gain an introduction. Delves's superficial charm and hidden vices suggest that the fictional George Wickham and John Willoughby in Jane Austen's novels were well-observed portrayals.

Mary Ann did not submit any defence to Delves's claim for £2,000 and by not doing so she admitted that she had broken a promise. She was told to pay one farthing in damages. Had she defended the claim, his tissue of lies was proof of bad character, entitling her to plead justification for her breach. Several other women who discovered their fiancé's true character after becoming engaged succeeded with this defence.

Women who were pressurised into an engagement were protected by juries when damages were assessed. James Nicholson of Newcastle received a farthing in March 1850. He claimed the costs of furnishing a large house, buying a ring and procuring the marriage licence after Mary Parkin, the orphaned daughter of a successful tailor, refused to go through with the wedding and married her childhood sweetheart instead. Mary had inherited her father's property and a junior lawyer conducting Nicholson's case was foolish enough to contend that he had lost a financially advantageous marriage. As the case progressed it became clear that Nicholson had set out to entice Mary from her first love, mariner Thomas Turnbull, whilst he was away at sea. On Turnbull's return Mary had support to end an engagement that she had been forced into by a determined older man.

As the year drew to a close, Frederick Strange attempted to claim damages from Mary Ann Pope, the daughter of a wealthy London tailor, who had briefly accepted him. Strange was reported to be old enough to be Mary Ann's father. He asked for substantial damages, and hoped that the court's verdict would be a lesson to young ladies that they could not make promises and then break them. He won a farthing in damages and had to pay his own legal fees, as the judge pointedly refused to make Mary Ann and her new husband liable for his costs.

There are striking similarities in these cases, which were decided at opposite ends of the country. Both women were just of the age of majority, lacking in life experience and considerably younger than the men who extracted a promise to marry and then gave their young fiancées the choice of honouring the engagement or handing over a substantial portion of their wealth to escape from it.

By 1860, jury verdicts showed that even where the parties were of similar age any designs on the property of a young woman would count against a man. Phoebe Hampton successfully defended a claim by Henry Hazeldene by demonstrating that he ended their engagement when he learned that her fortune had been settled in such a way that her future husband could not touch it. On discovering this, Hazeldene was reported to have drawn blood when he ripped a gold chain he had given to Phoebe from her neck and told her to 'go to hell', before storming out of the house.

Some fortune-hunters were older men who sought nothing other than a comfortable old age. For them, rich widows of mature years were the target. Such women usually proved very capable of looking after their property. Those who spent their married life supporting a husband as he built up a lucrative business were unwilling to share their financial assets with another man, except on their own terms. They knew to protect themselves by making an engagement conditional on the man having sufficient income of his own and using a marriage settlement to keep their wealth outside his control. Men whose ambition was for a prosperous retirement were usually happy to accept these conditions.

In 1797, James Atcheson, a 72-year-old retired button manufacturer from Shaftesbury, sued 50-year-old widow, Mary Baker who had a fortune of £24,000. The jury decided that she had made only a conditional promise to marry and rejected his claim. Atcheson obtained a retrial because he had disposed of his business, worth £300 a year, to meet her condition of marrying a gentleman, not a tradesman. Mary produced a new defence to the second jury, contending that she was free from any promise to Atcheson because she had discovered that he suffered from a disorder of the chest which left him unfit for a life of matrimony. When Atcheson's lawyer revealed that Mary had abandoned the elderly manufacturer for a young distillers' clerk of superior vigour, the outraged jury awarded Atcheson £4,000. This appears to be the highest award of damages in the eighteenth century. Surprisingly, the case received little notice in the press, suggesting that this level of damages was not out of the ordinary.

Mary declared that she would rather live permanently at the Court of the King's Bench than pay Atcheson anything. She appealed for the verdict to be struck out because of a defect in the paperwork in which Atcheson had set out his claim. In case this failed, she arranged to transfer most of her fortune to John Shaw, the former distillers' clerk, to whom she became engaged also on the condition that he gave up his employment so that she could marry a gentleman. Her appeal was successful. To avoid a further claim from Atcheson, she agreed to pay him an annuity of £200 a year for life and turned her energies to recovering her money from Shaw, who would not hand it back, arguing that it was an unconditional gift to him. Mary saw Shaw in his true colours and her infatuation with him promptly ended, but she strung him along with promises of marriage until he returned her property. She then refused to have anything more to do with him.

To set up a claim for breach of promise, Shaw wrote and requested that she meet him at church the next day to be married. Mary countered this strategy by deliberately misunderstanding his instructions and went to a different church, where she pretended to wait in vain for him. Shaw then also brought a claim for breach of promise, hoping to receive compensation for the salary he had given up at her behest. Mary, now reporting that she was almost 70, defended his claim by arguing that her own health was too frail for marriage. After two hours of deliberation, the jury accepted that poor health absolved her from the promise to marry. As a result Shaw lost his case and received nothing.

Mary was the first of a series of feisty widows who found themselves in court. In 1819, Widow Packwood was told to pay £20 for deserting Mr Gibbs, who claimed to be utterly indifferent to her £600 a year as he had property of his own. He alleged that he was the second man she had jilted and that the court had seen fit to award the previous suitor substantial damages. He hoped that the jury's verdict in his case would be a warning to all widows not to make and then break matrimonial promises. Instead, the jury set a marker of £20 for a wealthy widow to pay for the privilege of changing her mind.

More than a generation later, in 1864, a courtroom in Leeds descended into uproar when 50-year-old William Lister sued three times widowed Patience Wray, aged 70 but reputed to look much younger, for £1,000 and walked away with a farthing. Lister's claim was so consistently ridiculed by Mr Justice Blackburn that the *London Review* commented that partisan descriptions of Lister as a fortune-hunter would have warranted his legal team requesting another judge. Lister was a canvas dealer and apparently of a similar social and financial standing to Patience's previous husbands, who had included an upholsterer and a printer. The only significant disparity was her age, which she had concealed during the courtship.

In court, Patience's barrister portrayed her as a foolish old woman who had been prevented from making a very serious mistake when her nephew and heir arrived and convinced her to change her mind on the morning of the wedding. This misrepresented Patience, who was sufficiently astute to ensure that the bulk of the capital accumulated from her three husbands was secured to herself as part of the marriage settlement. Nor did the experience of being sued deter her from marriage. Little more than a year later she changed her name to Blackburn when she wed a man of her own age, a retired farmer from Knaresborough, North Yorkshire.

It is not known when Patience met Joseph Blackburn or whether there is anything beyond co-incidence that his surname was the same as that of the judge. If there was any connection then it might explain the extraordinary behaviour of his Lordship, who was rebuked by Lister's counsel for expressing the hope that the jury would reward Lister with insulting damages.

In 1880, George Fowke, the impoverished younger brother of a baronet, sued 60-year-old Charlotte Hornby, alleging that she had kept him dangling for eight years and then cast him off when the best years of his life were gone. Charlotte, who enjoyed an income of £5,000 a year, acknowledged a brief engagement in 1872, which she had ended when her enquiries about Fowke's means elicited the not-unsurprising news that he had none. Afterwards the couple remained companions, but with no renewal of the promise to marry. In summing up, the judge gave a glimpse of social conventions as they applied to older widows, stating that Charlotte's age protected her from any inference of an engagement to a man she had spent time with. He suggested that her money provided the incentive for the defendant to hang around her. Fowke lost his case as the jury decided that there was no promise to marry.

These courtships demonstrate that throughout the nineteenth century a widow with independent means was permitted considerable latitude in her conduct with the opposite sex. Few eyebrows seem to have been raised by a rich widow enjoying a close relationship with a man and no-one thought that this excluded her from the social milieu to which she belonged by her wealth and the past occupation of her husband.

A handful of men claimed their motivation in bringing a case for breach of promise against a woman was to vindicate their honour, though in some cases this was an attempt to divert attention from appearing mercenary. In 1855, John Holder, a captain in the Lancashire militia, sued Agnes Josling to establish that he had not acted improperly towards a lady. Holder proposed and was accepted whilst Agnes was raw with grief after the deaths of her parents. When she confessed a few days before the wedding that she had no affection for Holder, her brother advised her to end the engagement.

Holder claimed more than £400 for wedding preparations, visits to Agnes and the cost of the presents he had given to her during the courtship. The jury only awarded him £300 and the judge added to his discomfort by pointing out that the price of protecting his honour was the laughter of a crowded court and the ridicule of people throughout the Empire who would read of his actions in the newspapers.

Occasionally a woman or her family behaved in a manner that left a man with no option but to vindicate his character in public. In 1861, John Lomax sued Louise Norton. Her father insisted on defending the action and stated that Louise was justified in breaking her promise as she had believed Lomax to be a man of chaste and modest habits, but then discovered he was not. Lomax said that he would willingly have released her from their engagement, had he been asked, and had reluctantly brought the case to clear his character of the allegations being spread about him by her family. The judge eventually prevailed upon Louise's very stubborn father to settle the dispute without involving the jury, pointing out that he might come to regret the harm to his daughter if the jury decided against her. Lomax accepted an arrangement which involved the Norton family withdrawing the malicious statements about him and took no money from Louise.

Revenge was the prime motivator for a small number of men. In 1833, a staid Ayrshire schoolmaster, Peter Marshall, provided considerable mirth for a jury when he detailed the cost of each of the 39 presents he had given to Margaret Jack in the 11 years before her marriage and requested her to return those she had not already given back. The gifts included feathers, buttons and ribbons, some of which had worn out and been thrown away. Marshall pointed out that he had returned all her gifts to him, including a pin which was crooked with use. The jury accepted Margaret's plea that she had never promised to marry the schoolmaster and therefore that any items still in her possession were unconditional presents.

The attitude of juries towards breach of promise claims brought by men changed towards the end of the nineteenth century. In 1892, a jury at Chester told Mary Birch to pay damages of £50 to Albert Timmis, after hearing that if a woman had brought a case with the same facts she would have won. Montagu Leighton sued Hannah Simmons in 1900 for the return of jewellery he had given her shortly before she broke their engagement and married Emil Mendelsohn. The judge ruled that the items were unconditional gifts, but when he confirmed that Hannah had breached her promise to marry Leighton, she decided to settle the case and gave them back rather than let the jury decide what damages she should pay.

In the first decade of the twentieth century, two men on the make won more than nominal damages. Whilst the rise of the women's suffrage movement and claims for equality may have induced juries to consider claims from men in a different light, a more sinister reason may be that both women had foreign connections. In 1903, a London bicycle salesman, Frank Knight, was awarded £250 from Constance Ricardo. He claimed to have spent £30 preparing for marriage before releasing her from their engagement at her request because her mother was in poor health. A few weeks later he discovered that she had married someone else. Knight was portrayed in court by Constance's father as a fortune-hunter and the judge indicated that appropriate recompense could be provided by a single coin.

The year 1910 saw a claim by an impoverished 25-year-old haberdasher's assistant, Charles Bower, against a 54-year-old widow, Jesusa Ebsworth, who was ordered to pay him £100. The money was sufficient to keep him in the style he wanted to become accustomed to for six months. Jesusa gave notice of an appeal against the verdict but, faced with the court costs, she seems not to have proceeded.

If the tide did turn it was only for a short period. In 1915, William Gars took Fanny Land to court to teach her a lesson for treating him as a fool, after she proposed to him and then changed her mind. Fanny treated his action with levity also, not bothering to turn up in court to explain herself. The case went against her and she was required to pay a farthing.

The cause of all male plaintiffs was struck a death blow in 1917, when an action brought by French Viscomte Marcel Vigier, against actress Pansy Smith, incurred the odium of the legal system and the country. The wealthy Vigier stressed that he was not asking for damages but to vindicate his character, though he did ask Pansy to reimburse the money he had spent on her. His itemised bill consisted of 50 lunches at 15 shillings each, 75 dinners at 20 shillings each, 20 guineas for visits to the theatre and £10 for taxicabs.

The defence counsel and the judge commented harshly about Vigier wasting the time of a high court judge and 12 jurors when Englishmen were pouring out their blood on the battlefields of Flanders for the benefit of Vigier's country. The jury awarded him a farthing because there was doubt about whether awarding no damages was legal. Vigier was ordered to pay the costs of the whole action. This sent out a strong message to any future male plaintiff not to abuse the claim for breach of promise. Court action to recover damages from a woman was liable to leave a man substantially out-of-pocket and humiliated, whether he won the case or not. After the Vigier case, the only claims brought by men appear to relate to property disputes when an engagement ended. These had to be stated as breach of promise claims.

Although only a few actions against women were discussed in a public courtroom, it is likely that many claims of dubious merit threatened by fortune-hunters were settled by negotiation. It was unusual for a young, unmarried woman to feature in a breach of promise case brought by a man, suggesting that such claims were resolved out-of-court. A fortune-hunter who held letters written by a woman was in a strong bargaining position if she or her family wanted to prevent her indiscreet words being read in court and her reputation in a crowded marriage market being devalued. A private settlement would have been preferable to a fortune-hunter than a public court hearing, which might leave him substantially out-of-pocket and put people on their guard against him.

Married women, widows and older spinsters with means of their own were more likely to defend claims. They had less need to protect their reputation from the shadow of scandal and could face down extortion in court with the knowledge that the cost of doing so was likely to be little more than their own legal fees, even if the case went against them.

A few cases show how breach of promise could be used to blackmail a woman. In 1832, Sophia Pugh revealed that Henry Riches had threatened to publicise the circumstances in which she ended their engagement unless she paid him not to. He won his claim but received only a farthing, because bringing a court case in order to blackmail someone was an improper use of the legal process. In 1878, 'a being erect upon two legs and bearing all the outward semblance of a man', obtained £1,000 from a middle-aged spinster, Mary Ann Morris. During the lunch interval she agreed to pay Mr Heap this amount to settle his claim so that her gushing effusions in letters written over 20 years were not read out in court. The Caistor schoolmaster may be the only fortune-hunter to have profited from a breach of promise case once it came before a jury.

In 1914, Beach Chester, a respectable barrister, appeared to be threatening to use letters written to him by a Miss Soames for an unacceptable purpose, possibly to blackmail her father into buying them back. When Chester dropped his breach of promise claim the day before the scheduled hearing, Miss Soames's barrister asked the court to order him to return all her letters and any copies to prevent any malicious use ever being made of them.

The divergent nature of breach of promise claims for men and women resulted from the skilled oratory of eighteenth century barristers, who exploited polite society's view that well-bred women needed special protection from false lovers. They convinced lay juries that a jilted woman could never hope to recover from a broken heart or to find a man who would accept another man's rejects as his wife, and that such women should receive high compensation for their suffering. There was no parallel argument to justify men receiving more than token compensation from women who changed their minds.

Whilst breach of promise actions were in a formative stage, it was clear to juries and legal professionals that the men coming forward with large claims were usually fortune-hunters. They had suffered no actual losses and were targeting hard-working couples or vulnerable females for their money. Such cases could not be allowed to succeed. The legal system responded to extortion by ensuring that breach of promise claims for men were always decided according to strict contract law. This ensured that men with legitimate claims for out-of-pocket expenditure could recover their losses, whilst those with speculative claims or who tried to misuse the legal system usually found themselves paying heavily for the privilege.

Conclusion

*It would be most mischievous to compel parties to marry
who could never live happily together.*
**(Comment made by Lord Mansfield in Atcheson v Baker 1796,
quoted by Law Commission Report No 26, in 1969)**

The spectre of breach of promise overshadowed amatory relationships, although, compared to the number of engagements formed between 1780 and 1970, a court hearing was comparatively rare. Estimates suggest that 3,000-4,000 cases may have reached court in this period, with the majority being heard towards the end of the nineteenth century.

Most women knew when they could bring a claim against an errant male and all but the most foolhardy or naïve men realised that breach of promise hung above their heads like the sword of Damocles if a woman could prove that they had raised and then dashed her hopes of marriage. Some grooms went unwillingly to the altar rather than face a financially ruinous claim and others made a private arrangement to escape from an engagement they no longer wished to honour. How many of the reluctant grooms found happiness in their marriage we can never know.

Part of the popularity of breach of promise, and the reason it endured for over 200 years, was because other branches of the law refused to acknowledge the varied problems that stemmed from failed emotional relationships between men and women. In the nineteenth century, when poor women lacked rights and the financial means to mount legal challenges to unjust situations, sympathetic judges gradually stretched the boundaries of breach of promise to give them a practical remedy in the form of damages, when property, inheritance or family maintenance law ignored the root cause of their plight.

Even when a woman had given a man her money, helped him to build a successful business with her unpaid work, or maintained him with her wages, she had no claim against his assets when the relationship ended unless she was his lawful wife. Unwed women who had given birth found that the parish could only compel the

169

father of their illegitimate child to pay a very small sum towards its support, even if he was wealthy and she had no earning capacity.

The disadvantage of addressing situations such as these through a claim for breach of promise was that the woman's remedy was at the discretion of the jury, and she had to jump through hoops in order to receive anything. Initially, she had to find the money to pay lawyers to argue her case and establish that a promise of marriage had been broken. Proving a proposal was not easy if a determined man with financial means chose to deny her allegation. If she convinced a jury that the defendant had promised marriage, her character became the subject of an informal assessment, based on the whim of the jurors rather than on any objective principles, to decide how much compensation she deserved.

Unusually for a legal claim, breach of promise was subjective in its approach, compensating the person rather than the injury sustained. Contemporaries and modern researchers have struggled to find consistent principles to explain decisions in breach of promise cases, and arguably there were only two. Men who claimed damages from a woman could recover their out-of-pocket expenses if she changed her mind, but only if they could demonstrate that their proposal had not been made to try to gain control of her wealth.

Middle-class ladies were entitled to generous damages because refined women were considered to have very sensitive feelings, and supposedly experienced great emotional distress if they were rejected by the man who had won their heart. They also suffered the indignity of a public insult to their reputation when a man refused to honour his pledge to marry. This gender and class-based approach was firmly established by the end of the eighteenth century, and remained unchallenged until the start of the twentieth, despite changes in other social values. Even in 1893, *The Guardian* argued that:

in the vast majority of cases, the unlimited right of action for breach of promise is an unmingled wrong. The class of person for whose benefit it was designed for the most part scorn to have or shrink from having their injuries dragged into the light of a court of law, submitted to forensic and judicial analysis and made the subject of pecuniary assessment. On the other hand, the average plaintiff in a breach of promise case, even if she is not an impostor, is at least a person for whose wrongs one farthing would be ample compensation.

Although the same editorial acknowledged that there were cases where breach of promise could provide a remedy for real injustice, it nevertheless considered that breach of promise plaintiffs were wasting the time of the courts, which would be better spent trying 'bona fide and substantial suits'.

***

Although the amount of compensation for a lost marriage was discretionary, juries appear to have treated some issues with a degree of consistency. A rough and ready logic can be discerned in their approach at various periods, suggesting that jurors were influenced by prevailing middle-class attitudes and reflected wider public opinion in their decisions. It is difficult to argue that any firm rules emerged, because of the number of exceptions that confound any suggestion, but the following may have guided courts and juries in their decisions at different points.

Jurors in Georgian times appear to have made the most effort to link damages to what a woman might have lost and, in doing so, set precedents for substantial awards. They established the concept that a lady should receive good compensation for her hurt feelings, as well as for any quantifiable losses she had suffered, and that a man who had behaved in an ungentlemanly manner could have exemplary damages awarded against him. These tenets were extended to other countries whose legal systems were rooted in English law, with high damages also being awarded in North America and countries in the British Empire. This contrasted sharply with the position in Europe, where a breach of promise claim was never particularly lucrative, as damages were restricted to the actual losses that a plaintiff had sustained by the promise being broken.

As the nineteenth century progressed and the middle-classes became concerned about the escalating costs of maintaining the poor, jurors may have been motivated to ensure that a woman should not be chargeable to the parish because she had been let down by a man. Plaintiffs who had been seduced under a promise of marriage, and had an illegitimate child to support, received higher damages than those without children.

Worry about a woman becoming a drain on the poor rate may also explain why jurors upheld some very unlikely contentions by plaintiffs and awarded them a few pounds in damages. Transferring a small sum from a well-heeled man, who had perhaps not behaved as a proper gentleman should, to help a needy woman was a neat way of assisting her, even if it was outside the law. Most men escaping a breach of promise claim with damages they could afford to pay would have considered it a victory rather than a verdict to be overturned on principle.

Decisions by some Victorian and Edwardian juries appear to have involved class distinction. Ladies received ample compensation, irrespective of any injury sustained, and women who worked for a living generally obtained much less than those who aspired to dependant domesticity. One exception was 19-year-old Florence Joseph, a feather worker, who sued a London bookmaker with capital of £20,000 and earnings of £1,500 a year. She was awarded £1,500. In his summing up, the judge pointed out that although the defendant was rich the jurors should bear in mind the plaintiff's humble position in life and ignore any argument that her loss was greater than that of a better-off woman, clearly hinting that the jurors did not need to be generous to her.

Class distinction may also have applied to defendants. Men of limited prospects and resources were sometimes ordered to pay damages that substantially over-stated what the plaintiff had lost by not becoming a poor man's wife, whilst prosperous or powerful men enjoyed great, though not absolute, freedom to behave badly towards poor women. The vocal critics of breach of promise, who became obsessed with the delusion that all poor women used breach of promise as a way to extort money, handed unscrupulous men an easy defence. A number accused the discarded woman of blackmail, or contended that she had previously chosen to live as a mistress, to try to defeat her claim. Those who were unable to deny an offer of marriage could hope to escape with mild censure rather than a hefty bill, unless their conduct had been totally reprehensible.

In the early twentieth century, breach of promise entered yet another phase. As women were now claiming economic and social equality in all aspects of life, juries began to hold them much more accountable for their conduct during their engagement. Contemptuous damages were not new, but trivial sums were regularly awarded to deter the vengeful from bringing unreasonable cases. This meant that the claims reaching a jury were those involving a specific legal point, or where the defendant refused to negotiate a sensible compromise, or stood up to attempted blackmail.

During the mid-twentieth century, as women began to obtain better access to education and improved access to employment, breach of promise became an anachronism, even whilst it was still on the statute books. The speed with which women scorned to use it reflects just how irrelevant eighteenth century values were to the rock-n-roll age and the swinging sixties.

As the influence of social class began to weaken and externally imposed rules of conduct were replaced by more liberal attitudes, it became impossible to contend that a woman's character had been insulted and her chances of marriage ruined because a particular man refused to set a date for the wedding. In addition, the assumption in breach of promise claims that one party was wholly in the wrong, was at odds with the modern belief that when personal relationships broke down, the arrangements for separation should ignore fault and not compensate one party as a victim or punish the other for behaving badly.

When child maintenance was linked to a man's means and it was recognised that property disputes following a broken engagement, and maintenance for those in bigamous marriages could be transferred to other branches of law, breach of promise ceased to offer any benefit to the majority of women. Had it survived it would have been only a weapon for gold-diggers, extortioners and the vindictive to exact money or revenge, either in court or by private arrangement. Women, the usual beneficiaries of breach of promise claims, acknowledged that it is impossible to prevent feelings changing and unwise to enter into a life-long union if one party has doubts about the wisdom of taking that step. Improved opportunities for women to work in a range of careers meant that marriage was no longer their best chance of financial security, and most now considered the temporary pain of a broken engagement preferable to life in an unhappy marriage.

It is less than half a century since a refusal to marry ceased to be a cause for legal action. Although the threat of court proceedings for breach of promise entwined itself into the social fabric for more than a century, its traces are already as hard to locate as Dr Beeching's axed railways. Henry Joy, architect of Bournemouth's Victorian shopping mall, is commemorated by a blue plaque, and remembered as a local entrepreneur of vision. His 'mean, malignant and injurious' conduct towards Elinor Miller receives no mention. When Mary Elizabeth Smith tried to ensnare Earl Ferrers in a web of lies it was predicted that the case would be 'handed down to posterity as one of the causes celebres of Europe', yet few now know of her fictitious claim, or the fascination it held for Victorian society for many years.

Several defendants in breach of promise cases went on to fame, fortune, or notoriety and now have web-pages devoted to their lives and achievements, but it is rare to find any reference to the claim made against them, or the woman they jilted. Following the lead of Victorian and Edwardian writers, modern novelists and dramatists who set their work in these eras ignore breach of promise in their plots, despite the dramatic potential of the scenario.

The concept of claiming damages for a broken engagement is already so alien to modern understanding that the few surviving vestiges in *The Pickwick Papers* and *Trial by Jury*, seem only to confirm the good sense of those late-Victorians who declared that breach of promise was all about the greed and opportunism of avaricious women. That scores of decent, respectable and poor women were forced to bear the embarrassment of exposing their feelings in public because an amoral defendant had caused them financial loss or harm, no longer weighs on the scales of justice.

The concept of breach of promise of marriage, and the rules by which it was played out in the legal system, were developed by privileged and powerful men in an age where women had few legal rights. Georgian judges, barristers and jurors decided that the public honour of well-bred young ladies must be vindicated and that women who had been left holding the baby deserved financial compensation from its father.

Allowing these plaintiffs to obtain damages for a broken engagement beyond any out-of-pocket losses, opened Pandora's box and released the deadly sins of human nature. Greed, opportunism, revenge and fraud were never intended to fuel a successful bid for damages but when self-interested lawyers latched on to the claim they made it available to any woman who had been jilted by a man and, on occasion, to hussies who had not. The upper-class judges who mistakenly accepted that refined young ladies were tender creatures deserving special consideration, inadvertently dealt all women the upper hand in amatory arguments and some women used breach of promise to devastating effect to better their prospects at the expense of a man who had fallen foul of the idiosyncrasies of an unusual law.

In an age when men usually held all the aces, who can criticise any woman for playing to her own advantage when she discovered that in this game she could call the shots?

Appendix 1

Notes for Family Historians

The main primary source for breach of promise cases is newspaper coverage. Searchable newspapers are available on-line, either by personal subscription, or via a public library.

The best search term is 'breach of promise', as reports did not always mention marriage. Unfortunately, it can also produce many references not related to marriage. If the results are unwieldy, narrow down by searching for 'marriage' or a name or place.

Local or provincial newspapers often included more detail than national ones. If these papers are not searchable on-line, the only way is to trawl microfiche copies in an archive or library. This can be time-consuming and may not be worthwhile on a speculative basis, as newspaper reports often have insufficient detail to confirm that a person is an ancestor. If you need to search microfiche, find out when the local Assize Courts were held as this should narrow down the editions you need search. Some people had the case heard in an area you would not expect. Particularly interesting cases were regularly covered by newspapers serving unrelated parts of the country.

If you find a case in one paper, check other local and national ones. Some papers included much more detail, or interpreted the evidence differently. One report might present the plaintiff as a helpless victim and the defendant as a heartless cad, whilst another will show her as a scheming vixen and the defendant as an ensnared innocent.

Treat any comments about a woman's beauty and virtues, or a man's villainy or poverty, with scepticism. This was standard legal rhetoric employed by barristers to try to influence the amount of damages in favour of their client.

If you discover a breach of promise case in the family, it may be possible to research further. Some court papers have survived at

The National Archives (*www.nationalarchives.gov.uk*) and a few solicitors have deposited papers with local records offices. On-line resources, such as Access to Archives (*www.nationalarchives.gov. uk/a2a*), should be able to assist in locating anything available.

In the eighteenth and nineteenth centuries, some high-profile cases were written up and sold in pamphlet form. Some pamphlets have been digitised and can be accessed on-line.

A list of cases referred to in this book is included in Appendix Four and other authors listed in my bibliography provide similar lists in their books. These secondary sources can be a useful starting-point for checking surnames.

Appendix 2

NOTES FOR RESEARCHERS

The data sample of 1,124 cases was obtained primarily from newspaper reports of breach of promise claims 1780-1940, relating to England and Wales (I have defined a decade as 1841-50, 1891-1900 etc.):

	Number of Plaintiffs	% of Total Plaintiffs
Female Plaintiffs		
Women winning their claim	855	79.9%
Women losing their claim	110	10.3%
Women settling their claim	105	9.8%
Total female plaintiffs	1,070	100.0%
Male Plaintiffs		
Men winning their claim	36	66.7%
Men losing their claim	16	29.6%
Men settling their claim	2	3.7%
Total male plaintiffs	54	100.0%

Within the text I have also drawn on a few cases not analysed in the database. These include cases heard after 1940, cases heard in Scotland, cases where the press did not report the damages awarded, claims settled before court proceedings were instigated and some cases alluded to in hearings for debt or criminal activity.

Owing to the prominence given by newspapers to cases brought by men, it is considered that the number of cases identified will be much closer to the complete data set than for claims brought by women.

Average damages for female defendants (1780-1940)

Mean average (as awarded by juries) £364.69
Mean average (adjusted for appeals where known) £356.69
Median average £150
Mode average £100

Average damages for male defendants (1780-1940)

Mean average (as awarded by juries) £78.18
Median average £5.25
Mode average 1/4d. (one farthing)

At my discretion, I am willing to discuss my findings with researchers with a demonstrable interest in this topic.

Appendix 3

Money Matters

The value of money changed over the period. The average damages per decade, as awarded by a jury, when rebased to 2012 values using the Bank of England Inflation Calculator are as follows:

	£	£
1791-1800	292.86	28,044.27
1801-1810	640.59	48,684.94
1811-1820	1099.79	90,789.96
1821-1830	384.66	32,311.44
1831-1840	317.06	30,668.34
1841-1850	205.63	20,300.13
1851-1860	326.80	29,804.16
1861-1870	390.06	39,318.04
1871-1880	247.84	24,217.70
1881-1890*	271.22	29,852.90
1891-1900**	264.31	29,776.85
1901-1910	244.38	25,163.65
1911-1920	230.31	16,964.98

Excludes Knowles, whose damages of £10,000 were overruled on appeal.
**Excludes Mavro and King, who both obtained £4,000 in 1900, through claims involving child maintenance and a wealthy man.*

The rebasing has been calculated from the middle of the relevant decade.

Old Money

Damages in English breach of promise cases pre-date decimal currency. The former units of currency were Pounds (£), Shillings (s) and Pence (d).

£1 = 20 shillings

1s = 12 pence

A penny could be split into four. This coin, the farthing, was the smallest available.

Appendix 4

Partridge v Woosnam (1881) 80
Peake v Wedgwood (1826) 55-6
Pilbeam v Clemence (1882) 87, 141-2
Pilcher v Hawkins (1872) 38
Pizzey v Boulter (1821) 156
Potts v Lancaster (1895) 58
R v Cook (1920) 129
R v Francis (1914) 117
R v Grand and Demay (1889) 127
R v Kempshall (1897) 131, 134
R v McGill (1842) 126
R v Polombi (1901) 122
R v Reynolds (1886) 129
R v Watson (1904) 128
Redhead v Banks (1875) 90
Reeves v Joplin (1867) 81
Reynaud v Martin (1919) 111
Riches v Pugh (1832) 167
Ricketts v Gaskell (1903) 42-3
Ridley v Stirkazer (1858) 82
Roberts v Mayell (1899) 125
Rooke v Conway (1842) 28
Rose v Ollier (1824) 58
Ross v Levy (1884) 106
Rowley v Acres (1828) 63
Samwans v Winch (1893) 55
Sands v Sayer and Wife (1793) 157
Savage v Thacker (1920) 77
Sayer v Fuller (1900) 128
Scott v Wickenden (1827) 20
Sealy v Creed (1896) 68-9
Settle v Crumbleholme (1818) 13
Sewell v Strange (1900) 53
Seymour v Gartside (1822) 156
Sharpe v Duffus (1915) 44
Shaw v Baker (1800) 161-2
Shepherd v White (1893) 69
Shuttleworth v Kirkman (1864) 150
Simpson v Timperton (1828) 23
Smith v Clapham (1868) 88
Smith v Colton (1847) 114

Smith v Ferrers (1846) 112-4, 141, 174
Southerton v Byrne (1802) 10
Spenser v Cole (1819) 19-20, 58
Spicer v Moss (1865) 37
Spiers v Hunt (1907) 109-11
Storey v Eagle (1802) 11
Strange v Pope (1850) 160
Sutton v Lucas (1878) 60
Sutton v Pearce (1921) 44
Taylor v Woodhead (1863) 104
Thomas v Shirley (1862) 106-7
Thompson v Bush (1886) 87
Thorpe v Bright (1866) 67
Timmis v Birch (1892) 164
Townsend v Syms (1847) 28
Tredwell v Flack (1873) 53
Turner v Dennis (1817) 63
Turner v Rollinson (1834) 75
Tyndall v Short, (1873) 143
Vaughan v Albridge (1801) 58, 68
Valentine v Scanlon (1934) 77-8
Vigier v Smith (1917) 165
Wadsworth v Brighouse (1874) 79
Want v Hunt (1834) 104
Watson v Fitzhugh (1904) 128
Weaver v Forsyth (1828) 59
Webber v Symes and Wife (1850) 50-1
Webster v Williams (1874) 149
Weidermann v Walpole (1888) 108-9
Wells v Hooker (1891) 114
Wharton v Lewis (1824) 58
Whalley v Ellis (1894) 125-6
Whittam v Smith (1823) 23
Wilde v Atherton (1838) 118
Williams v Haines (1875) 70
Williams v Staples (1886) 975
Wood v Gartside (1857) 148
Woodley v Pickburn (1869) 101
Wright v Weekes (1827) 141

Appendix 5

Glossary of Legal Terms

Attorney	a former term for a solicitor.
Barrister	an advocate who represents a client in court hearings.
Civil Law	any law dealing with disputes between two parties where the rights of one have been infringed. Sanctions placed on the transgressing party are restricted to damages.
Contract Law	a branch of law dealing with broken agreements between two parties.
Criminal Conversation	a claim for damages made by a married man against his wife's lover.
	Despite its name, it was a civil dispute.
Criminal Law	a branch of law dealing with crimes committed by one person against another. It can issue fines or impose prison sentences.
Decree Nisi	a Court's agreement that a marriage can be ended by divorce on a specified date.
Defendant	a person who defends a claim made against him in court.
Judge	a legally qualified person who oversees proceedings in a court, ensuring that the law is followed. Very experienced judges may be asked to preside in appeal courts or to determine points of law

Jury	a group of 12 people who are not legally qualified, who listen to the evidence in a case and decide its outcome.
Lawyer	A generic term for any professionally qualified legal advisor.
Plaintiff	person making a claim in a civil court.
Sergeant-at-law	an advocate who represented a client in proceedings in certain courts during the nineteenth century.
Solicitor	a legal advisor responsible for most aspects of a client's claim, other than representing the client in court.
Tort Law	a branch of law dealing with cases where one party has harmed or injured the other.

Bibliography and Sources

Statutes and Official Reports

Evidence Act 1843
Evidence (Further) Amendment Act 1869
Law Commission Report No 26 Breach of Promise of Marriage 1969
Legal Reform (Miscellaneous Provisions) Act 1970
Marriage Act 1754

Printed Sources

Chitty, Joseph, *A Practical Treatise on the Law of Contracts (Section 111 Of a Contract to Marry)*, (London, 1841)
Frost, Ginger S, *Promises Broken-Courtship, Class and Gender in Victorian England*, (University of Virginia Press, 1995)
Lettmaier, Saskia, *Broken Engagements-The Action for Breach of Promise of Marriage and the Feminine Ideal*, (Oxford University Press, 2010)
McColla, Charles J, *Breach of Promise Its History and Social Considerations*, (Pickering and Co, 1879)
Steinbach, Susie *Women in England 1760- 1914 A Social History*, (Orion, 2005)

Novels and Plays

Austen, Jane, *Sense and Sensibility* (1811)
Austen, Jane, *Pride and Prejudice* (1813)
Bronte, Charlotte, *Jane Eyre* (1847)
Dickens, Charles, *The Pickwick Papers* (1837)
Dickens, Charles, *Great Expectations* (1861)
Gilbert, William, *Trial by Jury* (1875)
Thackeray, William, *Vanity Fair* (1847)
Trollope, Anthony, *The Last Chronicle of Barset* (1867)

Pamphlets and Periodicals

Annual Register 1780
Edinburgh Annual Register 1808-26
Maria Foote v Joseph Hayne 1824
Mary Elizabeth Smith v Earl Ferrers 1846
Edith Barber v Robert Fenton 1863

Principal Newspapers

The Guardian
The Observer
The Times

Principal Web Sites

A History of Wallasey: *www.historyofwallasey.co.uk*
Bank of England: *www.bankofengland.co.uk/education/Pages/inflation/calculator*
Old Bailey Online: *www.oldbaileyonline.org*

Other Online Sources (various providers)

Birth, Marriage and Death Registers
Census Returns 1841-1911
Parish Records
British Newspapers

Index

Discover the forgotten world of nineteenth century female miners in Denise Bates' debut book

Pit Lasses
Women and Girls in Coalmining c1800-1914

Women have long been recognised as the backbone of coalmining communities, supporting their men. Less well known is their key role as the industry developed, moving coal underground as well as running a home and bringing up a family.

When an government investigation into child labour in 1842 discovered that ungodly and undomesticated women and girls worked topless alongside naked men, public fury erupted and women were hastily banned from underground toil, to protect them from moral corruption.

The report has been neglected as a historical source, and information from 400 female workers about their lives has been ignored for 170 years. Based on their evidence, Pit Lasses examines the social and economic reality of females working underground, drawing out the largely untapped evidence within contemporary sources and challenging long-standing myths. Did women really work topless, or did the investigators have an ulterior motive for reporting as they did?

Pit Lasses adds enormously to our understanding of the role of women in coalmining, as well as shedding new light on Victorian society and its values.

Lancashire Evening Post

An eye-opening, even quite shocking read, illuminating as it does, an aspect of Victorian life that mainstream social histories have hitherto largely overlooked.

Jarrow and Hebburn Gazette

This book gives a fascinating insight into the hardships faced by the Pit Lasses as they struggled to earn a living and look after their families.

Tameside Reporter

This comprehensive exploration of the subject is a revelation

Doncaster Family History Society

Published by Pen and Sword Books